Dominating Client
Attraction

Book 1

The Path to Prosperity Series

Strategic advisor Board
Achieve Systems Pro

ISBN: 978-1-957217-65-9 (hardcover)
ISBN: 978-1-957217-66-6 (paperback)
ISBN: 978-1-957217-67-3 (ebook)

TABLE OF CONTENTS

INTRODUCTION

I remember sitting nervously across from my first potential big client. The weight of the moment was not just about closing a deal; it was about securing the future of my fledgling business. That day, I learned a vital lesson: Acquiring clients is not just a part of the business; it is the business. This realization hit me even harder when I later read that a staggering 90 percent of startups fail, and a lack of customer interest is often to blame. It underscored the critical importance of client acquisition in ensuring business success.

Client acquisition is the lifeblood of any business, big or small, new or established, local or global. It's a universal truth across all industries and locations. Without clients, there's no revenue; without revenue, a business cannot sustain itself, let alone grow. Attracting and converting prospects into customers who believe in your product or service enough to pay for it keeps the lights on and the doors open. It also fuels innovation, expansion, and the realization of entrepreneurial dreams.

THE PURPOSE OF THIS BOOK

The purpose of this book is straightforward yet ambitious: to arm you with the knowledge and tools essential for mastering client acquisition and fostering sustained business growth. In these pages, I've poured every lesson learned, every strategy tested, and every insight gained from my journey, aiming to bridge the gap between where you are now and where you aspire to be in the realm of business success.

Its unique approach, blending time-honored strategies with contemporary techniques to navigate the ever-evolving business landscape, sets this book apart. The business world is not static; it's a dynamic, ever-changing entity that demands adaptability and innovation. Recognizing this, I've tailored the content to provide a solid foundation in traditional client acquisition methods and introduce modern tactics that leverage digital advancements, social media, and the latest marketing trends.

This dual approach is designed to prepare you for the realities of today's business environment, equipping you with a versatile arsenal to attract and retain clients in a world where change is the only constant. Whether you're a seasoned entrepreneur or just starting out, the insights shared here aim to guide you through the complexities of client acquisition, helping you survive and thrive in the competitive business landscape.

THE IMPORTANCE OF CLIENT ACQUISITION

Understanding the critical role of acquiring new clients is fundamental to the success of any business. It's the fuel that powers the engine of growth, ensuring not just the survival but the thriving of your venture in a competitive landscape. Without a steady stream of new clients, a business risks stagnation, losing ground to competitors, and ultimately facing the threat of closure.

Attracting and retaining clients, however, is no small feat. It's a challenge that businesses of all sizes and sectors grapple with. I've encountered numerous hurdles in my journey, from identifying the right target market to crafting messages that resonate with potential clients. The digital age, while opening new avenues for client acquisition, has also introduced a host of new challenges, including increased competition and the need for a constant online presence. Moreover, retaining clients demands consistent delivery of value, exceptional customer service, and the ability to adapt to changing needs and expectations.

Mastering client acquisition strategies is not just about overcoming these challenges; it's about seizing opportunities to grow your market share, boost your revenue, and solidify your business's stability. Effective client acquisition strategies can transform your business, propelling it from obscurity into a recognized and trusted brand. It's about understanding your audience, leveraging the right channels, and delivering compelling value propositions that differentiate you from the competition.

Mastering these strategies is complex, requiring a blend of creativity, persistence, and strategic thinking. However, the rewards are undeniable. Businesses that excel in acquiring and retaining clients can achieve short-term gains and long-term success, establishing a foundation for stability and growth that can weather market fluctuations and shifts in consumer behavior. This is why client acquisition is essential for any business aiming for longevity and success in today's dynamic market environment.

KEY THEMES

In this book, we dive deep into the core themes essential for any entrepreneur looking to carve out a successful path in today's business world. Each theme is a building block, critical in its own right, but when combined, they create a robust framework for sustainable growth and success.

First, we tackle the foundation of any successful venture: defining and articulating a clear business strategy. It's about setting a course that aligns with your vision, values, and goals, ensuring every decision moves you closer to your aspirations.

Next, we delve into understanding and optimizing client acquisition costs. This is crucial for ensuring that the effort and resources invested in attracting new clients are done so efficiently, maximizing return on investment and fueling profitable growth.

Identifying and engaging with the target market is another vital theme. It's not just about knowing your potential clients but understanding them deeply—what drives them, their needs and preferences, and how best to communicate your value proposition to them.

Selecting and utilizing effective acquisition channels then becomes the next step. In a world brimming with options, from digital platforms to traditional media, choosing the right channels to reach your audience is paramount.

The significance of sales tactics and team building cannot be overstated. A skilled, motivated team and the right sales strategies are the engines of your client acquisition efforts, turning prospects into loyal customers.

Leveraging technology and content for growth is another theme we explore. In the digital age, technology and compelling content are powerful tools for attracting attention, engaging prospects, and converting them into clients.

The importance of customer retention and relationship building is also highlighted. Acquiring clients is just the beginning; nurturing those relationships and ensuring customer satisfaction is key to long-term success.

Last, we discuss utilizing social proof and referrals for exponential growth. In a world where trust is paramount, endorsements from satisfied clients can propel your business to new heights, creating a virtuous cycle of growth and success.

Together, these themes form the backbone of this book, offering a comprehensive guide to navigating the complexities of building and growing a business in today's competitive landscape.

WHAT YOU CAN EXPECT TO LEARN

As you turn the pages of this book, you're embarking on a journey to understand and master the art of building and growing a business. Here's a glimpse into the practical knowledge and actionable strategies that await you:

First, you'll learn to define and communicate your business strategy clearly. This isn't about lofty statements that sound good on paper but don't translate to real-world action. It's about crafting a strategy that's both visionary and executable, one that guides every decision and action within your business.

Next, we dive into the nuts and bolts of client acquisition costs—how to calculate them accurately and strategies for reducing them. This section is about efficiency and effectiveness, ensuring every dollar you spend on acquiring new clients works as hard as possible for your business.

Identifying and reaching your ideal customers can often feel like searching for a needle in a haystack. I'll share techniques that demystify this process, helping you find your ideal customers and engage them in a way that resonates deeply, turning interest into action.

Choosing and leveraging the most effective acquisition channels is critical in today's fragmented media landscape. You'll discover strategies for selecting the channels that best match your target audience and how to use them to your advantage, maximizing reach and impact.

Building a talented team and fostering a culture of growth and innovation are among the most challenging aspects of running a business. Insights shared in this book will guide you in assembling a team that's skilled and aligned with your business's core values and vision, driving your business forward. Content is king, but not all content is created equal. Tips for creating compelling content that drives demand and customer engagement will show you how to cut through the noise, capture attention, and engage your audience in meaningful ways.

Customer retention and maximizing lifetime value are where many businesses falter. The best practices outlined here will equip you with strategies for keeping your customers and delighting them, encouraging repeat business, and turning them into vocal advocates for your brand.

Lastly, setting up and running a successful referral program can turbocharge your growth. You'll learn how to harness the power of word-of-mouth, incentivizing your satisfied customers to become a driving force behind your client acquisition efforts.

This book is designed to be your guide, packed with practical advice, real-world examples, and actionable strategies. It's about moving beyond theory into the tangible steps you can take to achieve your business goals, laying the foundation for lasting success.

This book has been crafted with a singular commitment: to guide you through the intricate journey of growing your business by mastering the art of acquiring clients. It's a journey that requires patience, persistence, and a willingness to learn and adapt. But the rewards of this journey are immeasurable. By applying the strategies and insights shared within these pages, you're not just working toward increasing your customer base; you're building the very heart of a successful business.

Remember, the path to mastering client acquisition is ongoing. It's a path marked by continuous learning, experimentation, and refinement. But with each step forward, you're not only drawing closer to your business goals; you're also shaping a business that stands out, resonates with its clients, and leaves a lasting impact.

I hope this book serves as your compass, your beacon, guiding you through the complexities and challenges of client acquisition. May it inspire, enlighten, and empower you to achieve the success you've envisioned for your business. The journey of a thousand miles begins with a single step, and with the art of acquiring clients mastered, you're well on your way to making your business vision a reality.

1

DEFINING YOUR
BUSINESS STRATEGY

When I first grasped the concept of a clear business strategy, it was a game-changer for my venture. Before that moment, my approach to business was like sailing without a compass; I had a general idea of where I wanted to go but no concrete plan on how to get there. The realization hit me hard: without a well-defined strategy, I was at the mercy of the market's currents, reactive rather than proactive.

A clear business strategy is the blueprint of your company's future. It outlines where you want your business to go and how you plan to get there. This strategy becomes your roadmap, guiding every decision and action, ensuring they align with your ultimate goals. It's about making intentional choices and understanding that every step taken is a step toward a defined destination.

The power of a well-defined strategy cannot be overstated. It clarifies your vision, making it easier to communicate your goals and objectives to your team, investors, and customers. This clarity is infectious, inspiring confidence and commitment from everyone involved. With everyone pulling in the same direction, propelled by a shared understanding of the company's direction, the potential for success and growth skyrockets.

Moreover, a solid strategy allows for better resource management. Knowing your priorities means you can allocate time, money, and manpower more efficiently, focusing on activities that drive the most value. It also enhances your ability to anticipate and respond to changes in the market. With a strategy in place, you're not just reacting to competitors' moves but anticipating market trends and adjusting your course with agility.

However, perhaps the most significant impact of a well-defined business strategy is on growth. Growth becomes a deliberate, strategic effort rather than a byproduct of random actions. It's about setting ambitious yet achievable goals and then methodically pursuing them. This approach increases your chances of success and makes growth sustainable over the long term.

A clear business strategy is the cornerstone of any successful venture. It transforms ambition into action, guiding your business through the market's uncertainties toward success and growth. Reflecting on my journey, I realize that defining my strategy was the moment my business began to flourish. It was the moment I took control of my destiny, steering my venture with purpose and precision toward the future I envisioned.

UNDERSTANDING BUSINESS STRATEGY

When I finally got a handle on what business strategy meant, it was like a light bulb went off in my head. Before that moment, I used to think of strategy as just another business buzzword that sounded important but was just about making plans. But I learned that a business strategy is much more than that. It's the master plan that defines the direction of your business and outlines how you will achieve your goals. It's about making choices that position your business to win in the market.

Understanding the role of strategy in business success was a game-changer for me. It's not just about having a good product or service; it's about having a clear direction and a plan to get ahead of the competition and stay there. A solid strategy considers the big picture, including the market, your competitors, and your customers, and then it sets a course for navigating that landscape successfully. It guides your decisions and actions and keeps you focused on what's important for growing your business.

One of the key lessons I learned was the difference between strategy and tactics. For a long time, I thought they were the same thing. But they're not. Strategy is about the what and the why—what you want to achieve and why that's important. Tactics are about the how—the specific actions you will take to get there. For example, deciding to become the leading provider of eco-friendly products in your market is a strategic choice. The marketing campaigns, product developments, and partnerships you form to achieve that goal are your tactics.

This distinction between strategy and tactics helped me to organize my thinking and planning. It made me realize that before I could worry about the details of how to do some-thing, I needed to be clear on what I was trying to achieve and why. That's what strategy is all about. It's the foundation upon which everything else is built. Without a clear strategy, you might find yourself busy with many activities but not necessarily moving in the right direction. With a solid strategy, every effort and resource is aligned toward a common goal, making your business more focused, efficient, and, ultimately, more successful.

COMPONENTS OF A STRONG BUSINESS STRATEGY

When I sat down to hammer out what I wanted my business to be, I realized I was sketching the blueprint of my future. It wasn't just about making money or selling a product; it was about creating something that mattered to me and the world. That's when I understood the components of a strong business strategy weren't just items on a checklist; they were the DNA of my business.

First came the vision and mission statements. My vision was the dream I had for the business, the big picture of what I wanted it to become. It was like looking at the horizon and imagining the mark I wanted my business to leave on the world. The mission statement, on the other hand, was about today. It was my business's purpose, the reason it existed in the first place. Crafting these statements forced me to think deeply about what I was truly passionate about and what I wanted to achieve beyond making a profit.

Then, I dug into the core values and principles. These were the non-negotiables, the guiding stars that would influence every decision and action within the business. Whether it was integrity, innovation, or customer satisfaction, these values reflected what I stood for and wanted my business to stand for. They became the yardstick by which we measured every success and failure.

Setting long-term goals and objectives was next. This was where the rubber met the road, turning lofty visions into tangible targets. What did I want to achieve in the next year, five years, or decade? These goals had to be ambitious enough to push us but realistic enough to achieve. They were the milestones that would mark our journey toward the vision I had set.

Finally, I conducted a SWOT analysis—examining the strengths, weaknesses, opportunities, and threats related to my business. This was a reality check, a way to take stock of where we stood in the market and what we were up against. It helped me identify what we were good at and where we could leverage our advantages, but it also forced me to confront our shortcomings and the external challenges we needed to navigate.

Putting together these components of a strong business strategy was like assembling a puzzle. Each piece was crucial, and when they all fit together, they formed a clear picture of where my business was headed. It was a process that required honesty, introspection, and, sometimes, a willingness to accept hard truths. However, it was also incredibly empowering. With a solid strategy in place, I felt like I had a roadmap for the future that would guide my business through the market's uncertainties and toward the vision I had set out to achieve.

CRAFTING YOUR BUSINESS STRATEGY

Crafting my business strategy felt like navigating through uncharted waters. It was both thrilling and daunting. The first step was identifying my unique value proposition. I asked myself, "What makes my business different? Why would customers choose us over the competition?" It wasn't just about having a good product or service but about offering something truly unique that resonated with my target audience. This required a deep dive into what we could offer that no one else could, whether it was exceptional customer service, innovative products, or a unique approach to solving customer problems.

Next, I turned my attention to understanding my market and competition. This wasn't just about knowing who my competitors were but understanding their strengths and weaknesses, their strategies, and how they positioned themselves in the market. I also needed to deeply understand my customers' needs, desires, and pain points. This involved a lot of research, from surveys and focus groups to analyzing market trends and customer feedback. The goal was to find a sweet spot where my unique value proposition met the unaddressed needs of my target market.

Setting achievable and measurable goals was the next crucial step. It was tempting to aim for the stars, but I knew that goals needed to be grounded in reality. They had to be specific, measurable, achievable, relevant, and time-bound (SMART). This meant breaking down the big vision into smaller, actionable objectives that could be tracked and measured. For example, instead of a vague goal like "increase sales," I set a specific target to "increase online sales by 20% within the next 12 months through targeted social media marketing campaigns."

Finally, aligning the strategy with business operations was perhaps the most challenging part. It meant ensuring that every aspect of the business, from product development and marketing to customer service and supply chain management, was geared toward achieving the strategic goals. This required a top-down approach, where the strategy informed decision-making at every level, and a bottom-up approach, where feedback from operational levels could inform strategic adjustments. It was about creating a cohesive, agile operation that could move as one toward the set objectives.

Crafting my business strategy was a complex, iterative process. It required a clear understanding of what we stood for, a deep dive into the market and competitive landscape, realistic goal setting, and a commitment to aligning every part of the business with those goals. It was a blueprint for success, a roadmap that would guide us through the ups and downs of the business journey.

ARTICULATING YOUR STRATEGY

After crafting my business strategy, the next big challenge was articulating it clearly to my team. I knew that for the strategy to be effective, everyone in the organization needed to understand, believe in, and commit to it. This wasn't just about sending out a memo or holding a single meeting; it was about opening lines of communication and ensuring that the strategy became a part of our daily operations and culture.

Communicating the strategy started with a series of team meetings. I laid out the vision, the goals, and the plan to achieve them. But more than just talking, I focused on listening. I wanted to hear their thoughts, concerns, and suggestions. This wasn't just my strategy; it was our strategy. Ensuring every team member felt they had a stake in it was crucial for its success.

Ensuring alignment and commitment across the organization required more than just understanding; it required buy-in. I worked to tie the strategy to each department's and individual's roles, showing them how their daily tasks contributed to our larger goals. We set up regular check-ins to discuss progress and challenges and to celebrate wins—no matter how small. This ongoing dialogue helped keep the strategy at the forefront of everyone's mind and reinforced the idea that we were all together.

The role of leadership in championing the strategy was something I took to heart. I knew my team would look to me for guidance and inspiration as a model of the commitment I was asking of them. This meant being transparent about our challenges, being the first to adapt my approach when needed, and always being open to feedback. It also meant celebrating our successes and learning from our failures together. My role was to keep the momentum going, to keep us moving forward even when the going got tough.

Articulating the strategy was an ongoing process. It wasn't enough to communicate it once and then forget about it. It had to be part of our everyday conversations, decision-making processes, and company culture. It was about creating a shared vision that we were all committed to achieving, with leadership setting the tone every step of the way. This approach helped ensure that everyone was aligned with the strategy and fostered a sense of ownership and pride in what we were building together.

IMPLEMENTING YOUR STRATEGY

After laying out our strategy and getting the team on board, the real work began: implementing the strategy. This phase was all about turning our plans into action. It wasn't enough to know where we wanted to go; we had to map out the steps to get there and then start walking the path, one step at a time.

Breaking down the strategy into actionable steps was our first task. We took our overarching goals and broke them down into smaller, manageable tasks. This process was like planning a road trip. Our strategy was the destination, and now we needed to plot the route, including where we would stop along the way. Each task was assigned a timeline and a team member responsible for its completion. This approach helped us move from the abstract (our goals) to the concrete (the daily and weekly actions we needed to take).

Prioritizing initiatives and allocating resources was the next critical step. Not all tasks were created equal. Some were foundational, needing to be completed before others could start. Others were more impactful, promising to move us closer to our goals more quickly. We had to decide which tasks to tackle first and allocate our limited resources accordingly. This meant not just money but time and manpower, too. It was a balancing act, ensuring we were investing in the areas that would drive the most significant returns without spreading ourselves too thin.

Monitoring progress and making adjustments was an ongoing process. We set up regular check-ins to review our progress against our goals. These meetings were invaluable. They gave us a chance to celebrate our wins, which was always a boost. But more importantly, they allowed us to identify where we were off track and why. Not everything went according to plan. Some initiatives were more successful than we anticipated, while others fell flat. By closely monitoring our progress, we could pivot quickly, doubling down on what was working and rethinking what wasn't.

Implementing our strategy was a dynamic, iterative process. It required flexibility, resilience, and a willingness to learn and adapt. Sometimes, it felt like we were taking two steps forward and one step back. But every step was a learning opportunity, bringing us closer to our goals. This phase taught us that a strategy is not a set-it-and-forget-it plan but a living document that evolves with your business. It's about setting a direction, taking deliberate steps toward your goals, and being prepared to adjust your course as you learn what works best for your business.

EVOLVING YOUR STRATEGY

As we moved forward with our business strategy, it became clear that the ability to evolve and adapt was beneficial and necessary. The market didn't stand still, and neither could we. Our strategy had to be a living, breathing thing, capable of growing and changing just as we did.

Flexibility and adaptability in our strategy meant being open to change. It was about recognizing that what worked yesterday might not work tomorrow and that being too rigid could lead us to miss out on opportunities. This realization came to me not just from observing the market but from experiencing our own set of trials and errors. There were times when we hit the mark perfectly, and our strategy propelled us forward. But there were also times when we missed the mark, and our expected outcomes didn't materialize. Each success and failure was a learning opportunity to refine and strengthen our approach.

Learning from these experiences was crucial. Successes taught us what to replicate and build upon, while failures were often even more instructive, highlighting flaws in our assumptions or execution. It was important to dissect each outcome, understand its root causes, and integrate those insights into our strategy. This continuous learning process helped us stay aligned with our goals while navigating the ever-changing business landscape.

Knowing when and how to pivot our strategy was perhaps the most challenging aspect. Pivoting didn't mean abandoning our core vision or values; it meant adjusting our approach to better achieve our objectives. The decision to pivot came from closely monitoring our performance and being honest about what was and wasn't working. It could be sparked by a shift in customer behavior, a new competitor, or an unexpected opportunity. The key was to make these adjustments thoughtfully and deliberately, ensuring each pivot was a step toward greater alignment with our goals and market realities.

Pivoting our strategy required clear communication with the team, ensuring everyone understood the reasons behind the change and their role in the new direction. It also meant being prepared to reallocate resources, whether time, money, or manpower, to support the pivot. This agility became one of our greatest strengths, allowing us to seize opportunities and mitigate challenges more effectively.

In the end, evolving our strategy was about maintaining a balance between consistency and flexibility. It was about having a clear direction but being willing to adjust the sails when the wind changed. This approach didn't just help us survive; it helped us thrive, turning potential obstacles into stepping stones and continually moving us closer to our goals.

As we wrap up this chapter about the process of defining a business strategy, it's worth taking a moment to reflect on the key points we've covered. Crafting a business strategy is about more than just setting goals; it's about creating a roadmap for your business that outlines how you'll achieve those goals. It starts with understanding the core of what your business stands for, your vision, and your mission. It's about identifying what makes your business unique and leveraging it to stand out in the market.

We talked about the importance of knowing your market and competition, setting achievable and measurable goals, and ensuring that your strategy is woven into the fabric of your business operations. Communication, alignment, and commitment across your organization are crucial for bringing your strategy to life. And let's not forget the need for flexibility and adaptability—learning from successes and failures and being ready to pivot when necessary.

I want to encourage you to take that first step. Crafting a strategy that aligns with your vision and goals might seem daunting, but it's essential for your business's long-term success and growth. Start by asking yourself the tough questions: What do I want my business to achieve? Who are we now, and who do we want to become? What makes us different, and how can we use that to our advantage?

Remember, your business strategy is not set in stone. It's a living document that should evolve as your business and the market change. The important thing is to start somewhere. Use what you've learned to lay the foundation, then build on it, refine it, and let it guide you toward your goals.

Taking the first step in crafting your strategy is like setting sail on a voyage. There will be calm seas, rough waters, unexpected turns, and new horizons. However, with a solid strategy as your compass, you'll have what you need to navigate your business toward success. Take a deep breath, set your sights on where you want to go, and start charting your course. The journey ahead is yours to shape.

2

KNOWING YOUR NUMBERS

Understanding the numbers behind your business isn't just important; it's critical for success. It was a game-changer for my business when I first grasped the full extent of this truth. Financial literacy isn't about being able to crunch numbers or dazzle with accounting skills; it's about making informed decisions that drive your business forward.

Every entrepreneur needs to get comfortable with the basics of financial management. It's like learning the language of business. Without this knowledge, you're flying blind, making decisions based on gut feelings rather than hard data. And in the world of business, that's a risky strategy.

What are these key financial concepts and metrics you should know? First, there's the income statement, sometimes called the profit and loss statement. It tells you how much money your business made and spent over a specific period. It's where you see if you're operating at a profit or a loss. Understanding your income statement helps you pinpoint where you're making money and where you might be bleeding it.

Then, there's the balance sheet. This snapshot shows you what your company owns (its assets) and what it owes (its liabilities), along with the equity you and any other stake-holders have in the business. It's a crucial tool for assessing your business's financial health and stability.

Let's not forget about the cash flow statement. Cash flow is the lifeblood of your business. This statement tracks the cash coming in and going out of your business. Positive cash flow means you have more money coming in than going out, which is where you want to be. It's all about effectively managing your operating, investing, and financing activities.

Beyond these statements, there are key metrics like the break-even point, gross margin, net profit margin, and cash flow forecast. These metrics give insight into how much you need to sell to cover costs, the profitability of your products or services, and how much cash you'll have on hand in the future.

Financial literacy empowers you to make strategic decisions that can lead to growth and sustainability. It's about knowing where your money is coming from, where it's going, and how to plan for the future. For me, embracing these financial fundamentals was not just about survival but about setting the stage for long-term success.

UNDERSTANDING FINANCIAL STATEMENTS

Income Statements

When I first wrapped my head around the income statement, it was like a light bulb went off. This document, also known as the profit and loss statement, is a fundamental piece of the financial puzzle for any business owner. It's not just a sheet of numbers; it's a story of your business's performance over a specific period, usually a month, quarter, or year.

The income statement shows you how much money your business made (its revenue), how much it spent (its expenses), and what's left over (the net profit or loss). Understanding this document is crucial because it directly reflects the results of your business operations.

Reading and interpreting income statements can initially seem daunting, but once you get the hang of it, it becomes second nature. The top line is your revenue, the total amount of money brought in from sales before any expenses are subtracted. As you move down the statement, you'll see various expenses listed, such as cost of goods sold, operating expenses, and taxes.

The magic happens when you subtract all these expenses from your revenue. What's left is your net income, also known as your bottom line. This number tells you whether your business made a profit or suffered a loss during the period covered by the income statement.

However, the income statement offers more than just a snapshot of profit or loss. By diving deeper, you can identify trends in your revenue and expenses, assess your cost management, and evaluate the overall financial health of your business. For example, if your revenue is growing but your net income isn't, it might be time to look closer at your expenses.

Learning to read and interpret income statements has been invaluable in my journey. It's allowed me to make informed decisions about where to cut costs, when to invest in growth, and how to steer my business toward financial stability and success. It's a skill that every entrepreneur needs in their toolkit.

Balance Sheets

The day I truly understood the balance sheet was a turning point for my business. Think of the balance sheet as a snapshot of your company's financial condition at a specific moment in time. It's divided into three main parts: assets, liabilities, and equity. Each section tells a part of your business's financial story, showing what you own, what you owe, and what's left over for you and any other owners.

Assets are everything your business owns that has value. This can be cash in the bank, inventory, equipment, and even money owed to you by customers (accounts receivable). Liabilities are what your business owes to others—things like loans, accounts payable, and any other debt. Equity, sometimes called owner's equity or shareholders' equity, is what's left over when you subtract liabilities from assets. It represents the ownership interest in the business.

Analyzing the health of your balance sheet involves looking at these three components and understanding how they interact. A healthy balance sheet usually shows a solid base of assets funded by a mix of liabilities and equity. Too much debt compared to equity can be a red flag, indicating potential financial instability. On the other hand, a strong base of assets compared to liabilities can signal a healthy, thriving business.

One of the first things I learned to do was to assess the liquidity of my business by looking at the balance sheet. This means figuring out how easily we could turn assets into cash to cover short-term obligations. Another critical analysis involves understanding the company's solvency or its ability to meet long-term debts and obligations, which can give insights into the business's long-term viability.

Getting comfortable reading and analyzing a balance sheet has allowed me to make more informed decisions about investing in new projects, taking on debt, and managing the company's day-to-day financial operations. It's a powerful tool that helps me keep my finger on the pulse of my business's financial health, ensuring we're on solid ground today and well-positioned for future growth.

Cash Flow Statements
Getting a grip on the cash flow statement was like finding the missing piece in managing my business. This document is all about tracking the cash that flows in and out of your business

over a certain period. It's a straightforward concept, but its implications are profound.

Cash inflows are the money coming into your business. This could be from sales, investment income, or financing. Conversely, cash outflows are the money going out—expenses like rent, salaries, and payments to suppliers. The cash flow statement breaks these down into three main activities: operating, investing, and financing.

Understanding this flow of cash is crucial because it tells you if your business is generating enough cash from its operations to sustain itself, invest in growth, and manage its debts. A business can be profitable on paper, according to the income statement, but still face financial difficulties if the cash isn't there when needed.

The significance of cash flow in operational sustainability can't be overstated. Early on, I learned the hard way that running out of cash is one of the quickest paths to business failure. It doesn't matter how good your product is or how much your customers love you—if you don't have enough cash to keep the lights on, you're in trouble.

Monitoring the cash flow statement has become a regular part of my routine. It helps me plan for future expenses, decide when to make significant purchases, and determine if we can afford to expand. Perhaps most importantly, it gives me peace of mind. Knowing that our cash flow is healthy means I can focus on running the business rather than lying awake at night worrying about whether we can pay our bills.

In essence, the cash flow statement is more than just a financial document; it's a vital tool for ensuring the heartbeat of your business remains strong. It's taught me that managing cash flow effectively is not just about survival; it's about creating a foundation for sustained growth and success.

BUDGETING AND FORECASTING

Creating a Budget

Creating a realistic budget was a turning point for my business. It's like setting up a roadmap for where you want your business to go financially. At first, the process seemed overwhelming. However, I quickly learned that a budget is just a plan for your money, and having a plan is always better than flying by the seat of your pants.

The first step in developing a business budget is to look at your income. How much money is coming in each month? This includes all sources of income, not just from sales but also from investments, loans, and any other revenue streams. Knowing your total income gives you a starting point for how much you can afford to spend and save.

Next, list your expenses. This includes everything from rent and utilities to salaries, inventory costs, and marketing. Don't forget to include variable expenses that can fluctuate, like shipping costs or seasonal advertising. It was eye-opening to see where the money was going, and it helped me identify areas where we could cut back.

Once you have your income and expenses laid out, it's time to do some math. Subtract your expenses from your income to see if you're operating at a profit or a loss. This simple equation was my first reality check. It showed me whether my business model was sustainable or if I needed to make some changes.

Creating the budget is only the beginning. The real magic happens when you start using it to guide your business decisions. This means regularly reviewing your budget and comparing it to your actual business performance. If you're consistently overspending in one area, it's time to adjust your budget or spending. On the flip side, if you find you're consistently under budget, you might have room to invest more in areas that could drive growth.

Adjusting your budget based on business performance is crucial. It's not about sticking rigidly to the numbers but about understanding the financial health of your business and making informed decisions. For me, this meant sometimes cutting back on non-essential expenses to bolster our emergency fund or investing more in marketing during peak seasons to maximize revenue.

Ultimately, creating and adjusting a budget has been about taking control. It's a tool that has allowed me to confidently steer my business, knowing that a clear understanding of our financial situation backs every decision I make.

Financial Forecasting

When I first tackled financial forecasting for my business, it felt like trying to predict the weather. However, I quickly learned that forecasting wasn't about having a crystal ball; it was about making educated guesses based on the information I had. It became a crucial part of my strategic planning, helping me prepare for the future and make informed decisions.

Projecting future revenues and expenses starts with looking at past performance. I dug into my sales records, expense reports, and any patterns in the market. From there, I could make assumptions about how my business might perform in the coming months or years. For example, if I noticed an uptick in sales every summer, I could forecast a similar increase in future summers.

However, it's not just about repeating patterns. I also had to consider any changes in the business environment, like new competitors entering the market or changes in supplier costs. These factors could affect my revenues and expenses, so I included them in my projections.

Using these forecasts for strategic planning has been a game-changer. With a clearer picture of where my business might be heading financially, I could make strategic decisions about where to allocate resources. For instance, if my forecast showed that we were likely to have a surplus of cash, I might decide to invest in new equipment or marketing campaigns to drive growth.

On the flip side, if the forecast indicated a potential cash shortfall, I knew I needed to tighten our belts, perhaps by delaying non-essential expenses or finding ways to boost sales in the short term. This proactive approach helped me avoid financial pitfalls and stabilize the business.

Financial forecasting has also been invaluable in discussions with investors and lenders. Being able to show them where the business is now and where it's headed has been crucial in securing funding and support.

Financial forecasting is about preparing for the future, not predicting it with absolute certainty. It's given me the confidence to make bold decisions, knowing they're grounded in a thoughtful analysis of our financial trajectory. It's a tool that's helped me navigate the ups and downs of running a business, ensuring that we're always moving forward, even when the path ahead seems uncertain.

Managing Cash Flow

Strategies for Improving Cash Flow

Improving cash flow was a challenge I faced head-on in the early days of my business. It's like keeping the lifeblood of your business flowing smoothly, ensuring you have enough cash on hand to cover your expenses and invest in growth. Two strategies that made a significant difference for me were invoice management and expense tracking and reduction.

First, let's talk about invoice management. Initially, I was a bit casual about sending invoices and following up on payments. However, I quickly learned that lax invoice management could lead to serious cash flow problems. So, I started sending invoices promptly after a job was completed or a product was delivered. I also set clear payment terms upfront and followed up diligently on any late payments. Implementing an online invoicing system was a game-changer, making it easier for clients to pay and for me to track who owed me money. This simple shift helped cash come in more regularly, easing the financial squeeze.

Then, there's expense tracking and reduction. When money was tight, I looked hard at where it was going. I started by categorizing all my expenses, which helped me see exactly where my money went each month. This exercise was eye-opening. I found subscriptions I'd forgotten about, services we weren't fully utilizing, and supplies we could get at a better price elsewhere. By getting a handle on my expenses, I could make more informed decisions about where to cut back without sacrificing the quality of our products or services. For example, renegotiating contracts with suppliers or opting for more cost-effective marketing strategies helped reduce our expenses significantly.

These strategies didn't just improve our cash flow; they also taught me the importance of being proactive about financial management. By staying on top of invoices and expenses, I could prevent cash flow problems before they started rather than scrambling to fix them after the fact. It was a lesson in the power of prevention and the importance of keeping a close eye on the financial pulse of my business.

Recognizing Cash Flow Problems

Spotting cash flow problems early on was a skill I had to learn the hard way. It's like noticing the warning lights on your car's dashboard. Ignoring them can lead to a breakdown, and in business, that breakdown can mean running out of money to keep operations going. There are a few signs I've learned to watch for, and each has taught me valuable lessons on managing cash shortages.

One of the first signs of cash flow issues I encountered was delays in paying suppliers or bills. It was a red flag that our cash wasn't stretching as far as it needed to. Another warning sign was using credit cards or loans to cover operational costs regularly. While credit can be useful, relying on it for day-to-day expenses wasn't sustainable. I also noticed that when we were struggling to make payroll, it clearly indicated that our cash flow needed immediate attention.

Facing these signs head-on, I learned several solutions for managing cash shortages. The first step was always to revisit our budget and cut any non-essential expenses. It was surprising how much we could save by pausing or renegotiating certain services and subscriptions. Another strategy was to improve our invoicing process. By invoicing promptly and following up on late payments more aggressively, we could speed up our cash inflow.

I also explored different financing options. Lines of credit and short-term loans could provide a lifeline in tight situations, but I learned to use them wisely, ensuring we could meet the repayment terms without adding undue stress to our cash flow. Additionally, I found that offering discounts for early customer payments could encourage quicker inflows, helping us bridge the gap during lean periods.

Perhaps the most important solution was open communication with suppliers and creditors. By being upfront about our financial situation, we could often negotiate more favorable payment terms, giving us the breathing room we needed to get back on track.

Recognizing and addressing cash flow problems has become a critical part of my role as a business owner. It's about being proactive, staying vigilant, and always looking for ways to optimize our financial health. These challenges have taught me resilience and the importance of having a solid strategy for managing cash flow, ensuring that the business can survive and thrive in the long term.

PRICING STRATEGIES

Understanding Your Costs

I realized early on that all costs aren't created equal. They fall into two main categories: fixed and variable. Grasping this concept was crucial for managing my finances effectively and calculating my break-even points.

Fixed costs are the expenses that stay the same, regardless of how much or how little we sell. Think of them as the baseline expenses necessary to keep the doors open. For my business, this included rent for our space, insurance, and salaries for my core team. These costs were predictable, which made planning easier, but they also meant that there was a minimum amount of revenue we needed to generate each month, no matter what.

Variable costs, on the other hand, fluctuated with our level of production or sales. This included things like raw materials, shipping costs, and sales commissions. The more we sold, the higher these costs would go. But unlike fixed costs, variable costs could be scaled back during slower periods, giving us flexibility in managing our cash flow.

Calculating the break-even point became my next challenge. At this point, our total revenues matched our total costs, meaning we were neither making a profit nor taking a loss. Understanding this threshold was like finding the key to financial stability. It showed me how much we needed to sell to cover all our expenses and helped me set realistic sales targets.

To calculate our break-even point, I first totaled our fixed costs. Then, I looked at our average price per product and subtracted the variable cost per product to find our contribution margin per unit. Dividing our total fixed costs by this contribution margin gave me the number of units we needed to sell to break even.

This calculation was an eye-opener. It highlighted the importance of controlling both fixed and variable costs and showed me the direct impact of pricing and cost management on our profitability. By understanding our costs and break-even point, I could make informed decisions about pricing, budgeting, and growth strategies. It was a fundamental step in ensuring my business's financial health and sustainability.

Setting Prices

Pricing isn't just about covering costs; it's about understanding the value you offer and how you fit into the competitive landscape. Two approaches helped me navigate this: value-based pricing and competitive pricing strategies.

Value-based pricing was a game-changer for me. It's all about setting prices based on the perceived value of your product or service to the customer rather than just the cost to produce it. This approach required me to get into my customers' heads and understand what they truly valued about what we offered. Was it the quality? The convenience? The brand? By focusing on these aspects, I could justify a higher price point because the value to the customer was clear and tangible. It wasn't about being expensive; it was about being worth it.

Then there's competitive pricing, which required me to closely monitor what others in my market were charging. This didn't mean I had to undercut everyone else to win business. Instead, it was about understanding where my offerings sat in the spectrum of options available to my customers. Were we a premium option, or were we aiming to be the best value for money? By analyzing my competitors' pricing, I could position ours in a way that made sense to our target market and reflected our place in the industry.

Both strategies required a deep understanding of my customers and competitors. Value-based pricing pushed me to highlight what made us special, while competitive pricing ensured we remained relevant in our market. Together, they formed the backbone of a pricing strategy that supported our growth, covered our costs, and appealed to our customers. It was a delicate balance, but getting it right meant we could thrive in a competitive landscape.

FINANCIAL ANALYSIS AND HEALTH

Key Financial Ratios

When I first dove into the financial side of running a business, I felt like I was trying to read a foreign language. However, as I got more comfortable, I realized that understanding key financial ratios wasn't just useful but crucial for making informed decisions. Two types of ratios stood out to me: profitability ratios and liquidity ratios. They became my go-to tools for assessing the health of my business.

Profitability ratios were about answering one big question: Is my business making money? It sounds simple, but there's a lot that goes into it. I started with the gross profit margin, which showed me the percentage of revenue that remained after covering the cost of goods sold. It clearly indicated how efficiently we were producing and selling our products. Then, there was the net profit margin, which considered all expenses, not just the cost of goods sold. This gave me a more comprehensive view of our overall profitability, including how well we managed our operating costs and overhead.

Liquidity ratios, on the other hand, were about understanding if we had enough cash on hand to pay our bills. The current ratio was a lifesaver here. By comparing our current assets to our current liabilities, it showed me if we could cover our short-term obligations. This was crucial for ensuring we didn't run into cash flow problems. Another helpful metric was the quick ratio, which was similar to the current ratio but excluded inventory from the assets. It was a stricter measure, showing how well we could meet our liabilities with the most liquid assets.

These ratios did more than just give me numbers to track; they provided insights into how well the business was doing and where we could improve. Profitability ratios helped me see where we could be more efficient or where we might need to adjust our pricing strategy. Liquidity ratios alerted me to potential cash flow issues before they became crises, allowing us to adjust in time.

Learning to use these financial ratios was like learning to navigate with a compass. They didn't tell me exactly where to go, but they gave me the tools to find my way, ensuring that my business stayed profitable and sustainable.

Regular Financial Review

Getting into the habit of regular financial reviews was like setting up routine health check-ups for my business. At first, it felt like an extra task on my never-ending to-do list, but it quickly became one of the most critical habits for healthily maintaining and growing my business.

I started by setting aside time each month to dive into the numbers. This wasn't just a quick glance at the bank balance; it was a comprehensive review of our income statement, balance sheet, and cash flow statement. I looked at our financial ratios, checked our progress against the budget, and evaluated our financial health. These monthly check-ups helped me catch issues before they turned into problems and identify opportunities we were well-positioned to take advantage of.

But these reviews weren't just about looking at numbers. They were also about understanding the story behind them. Why did our expenses increase last month? Was it a one-time investment or a sign of rising costs? How did our profitability ratios change, and what does that say about our pricing strategy or cost management? This deeper analysis was crucial for making informed decisions.

I adjusted our strategies as needed based on what I learned during these reviews. Sometimes, this meant cutting unnecessary expenses or reallocating resources to more profitable areas. Other times, it involved changing our sales strategy or finding ways to improve our cash flow management. These weren't always easy decisions, but having a clear understanding of our financial health made it easier to determine the right course of action.

Regular financial reviews also prepared me for discussions with investors, lenders, and other stakeholders. I could speak confidently about our financial position, backed up by data and a thorough understanding of our financial health. This transparency and preparedness built trust and opened doors to new opportunities.

These regular financial check-ups became the backbone of our strategic planning process. They ensured that our strategies were grounded in financial reality, allowing us to pivot when necessary and double down on what worked. It was a discipline that turned financial management from a daunting task into a powerful tool for driving growth and ensuring long-term success.

TAXES AND LEGAL OBLIGATIONS

Business Taxes

Navigating the world of business taxes was one of the steepest learning curves I faced. Initially, it felt like a maze of regulations, deadlines, and forms that I couldn't afford to get wrong. Understanding my tax responsibilities and planning for liabilities became a crucial part of my business strategy, ensuring we stayed compliant and financially healthy.

First, getting a grip on the different types of taxes my business was responsible for was essential. There were income taxes on the profits, payroll taxes for my employees, and sometimes, sales taxes on the products we sold. Each type of tax had its own set of rules and deadlines. I quickly learned that staying on top of these details was non-negotiable. It wasn't just about paying taxes but understanding how these obligations impacted our cash flow and financial planning.

Planning for tax liabilities became a critical part of our financial strategy. I started setting aside a portion of our monthly profits into a separate account, specifically for taxes. This way, when tax season rolled around, we weren't scrambling to find the funds to meet our liabilities. It was a simple system, but it saved us from cash flow headaches and helped us avoid penalties for late or insufficient payments.

But more than just a financial strategy, planning for our tax liabilities was about peace of mind. Knowing that we were prepared for tax season, had accounted for our obligations, and wouldn't face unexpected debts allowed me to focus on growing the business. It was a clear reminder that understanding and managing taxes wasn't just a bureaucratic chore but an integral part of running a successful business.

In essence, mastering the basics of business taxes and planning for those liabilities was a crucial step in ensuring the stability and growth of my business. It was about more than just compliance; it was about making informed decisions that supported our long-term success.

Keeping Accurate Records

Keeping meticulous records for tax purposes became my unexpected ally. It wasn't just about logging every sale or expense but creating a reliable trail I could follow back at any time.

This practice proved invaluable during tax season, audits, or whenever I needed to make informed financial decisions. It was like having a detailed map of where my business had been financially, which helped me navigate where it was going.

I started with the basics: categorizing all transactions, keeping receipts, and using accounting software to track everything in real time. This software became my financial dashboard, giving me an instant overview of my business's health and simplifying tax filing. I also made it a habit to review and reconcile my accounts monthly, ensuring that every number in my books matched my bank statements and receipts.

Another best practice that paid off was setting up a separate business bank account. This move was a game-changer. It kept my personal and business finances distinct, making it easier to manage cash flow and document expenses accurately for tax purposes. Plus, it lent credibility to my business operations, showing that I was serious about managing my company professionally.

Perhaps the most crucial practice was regularly consulting with a tax professional. This wasn't just about outsourcing the complexity of tax laws; it was about gaining insights into leveraging tax advantages and avoiding pitfalls. Their expertise helped me navigate the ever-changing tax landscape, ensuring my record-keeping practices were up-to-date and compliant.

Adopting rigorous record-keeping practices transformed how I managed my business finances. It wasn't just about fulfilling a legal requirement but empowering my business decisions with accurate, timely information. This discipline around financial documentation became a cornerstone of my business's success, providing clarity, security, and peace of mind.

Wrapping up this chapter on the importance of knowing your numbers, I can't stress enough how crucial financial literacy has been to the success of my business. It's like navigating a ship; you must know how to read the stars. In the world of business, those stars are your financial metrics. Understanding these numbers has given me the confidence to make informed decisions, anticipate challenges, and seize opportunities with precision.

But mastering your business finances isn't a one-time achievement. It's an ongoing journey of education and adaptation. The financial landscape is always changing, with new regulations, market conditions, and opportunities always emerging. Staying ahead means committing to continuous learning. Whether it's brushing up on the latest tax laws, exploring new financial tools, or simply refining your budgeting skills, every bit of knowledge you gain solidifies the foundation of your business.

I encourage every entrepreneur to dive into the numbers, get comfortable with the uncomfortable, and see financial management not as a chore but as a powerful tool for growth. There are countless resources, from online courses and books to workshops and seminars, all designed to enhance financial literacy. And don't overlook the value of a good mentor or financial advisor. Their insights can be invaluable, offering shortcuts to best practices and helping you avoid common pitfalls.

Remember, knowing your numbers is more than just keeping your business afloat. It's about steering your venture toward its fullest potential. Take the time to educate yourself, embrace the numbers, and watch your business transform.

3

UNDERSTANDING YOUR MARKET

Understanding your market is like having a roadmap in the wilderness of business. It guides every decision you make, from product development to marketing strategies. Without this understanding, you're essentially wandering in the dark, hoping to stumble upon success. I learned this the hard way early in my entrepreneurial journey.

There was a time when I launched a new product line without conducting thorough market research. I was confident that the quality alone would win customers over. However, I overlooked a crucial aspect: my target market's preferences and needs. The product, while high-quality, didn't align with what my potential customers were looking for. Sales were dismal, and I was left with a significant inventory that nobody wanted. This experience was a wake-up call. It highlighted the stark difference between what I thought the market needed and what it demanded.

This failure taught me the undeniable value of deeply understanding your market. It's not just about knowing who your customers are but also understanding their challenges, preferences, and behaviors. This insight informs your product development, marketing messages, and even your business model. It's the difference between offering something people need and trying to convince them to want what you have.

After that misstep, I dedicated myself to learning everything I could about my target market. I conducted surveys, analyzed customer feedback, and closely monitored industry trends. This effort paid off when I relaunched the product line, this time with features and marketing that spoke directly to my customers' needs. The difference was night and day. Sales picked up, and the product line became one of the pillars of my business.

This experience underscored a fundamental truth: Understanding your market is not optional; it's essential for business success. It allows you to navigate the competitive landscape confidently and make decisions that lead to growth and profitability. Without it, you're just guessing, and in business, guesses can be costly.

THE BASICS OF MARKET RESEARCH

There are two main types of market research: primary and secondary. Primary research is all about collecting data firsthand. This means directly contacting potential or current customers through surveys, interviews, or even observing consumer behavior. It's like going out into the field and getting your hands dirty to understand what your customers want and need. For my business, conducting primary research involved sending out surveys to our email list and having one-on-one conversations with customers at trade shows. It was eye-opening to hear directly from them, and it gave me insights I couldn't have gotten any other way.

On the other hand, secondary research involves analyzing data that has already been collected by someone else. This could be looking at industry reports, studying competitor data, or reading published consumer surveys. It's like being a detective, piecing together clues to form a bigger picture of the market landscape. When I first started diving into secondary research, I spent hours reviewing industry reports and analyzing my competitors' marketing strategies. It helped me understand market trends and identify gaps in the market that my business could fill.

Conducting market research doesn't have to be complicated or expensive. For primary research, simple online surveys like SurveyMonkey or Google Forms can provide valuable customer insights. Social media platforms are also great for engaging directly with customers and getting their feedback. For secondary research, start with what's freely available. Government databases, industry associations, and even articles and case studies can provide a wealth of information.

In my journey, understanding the basics of market research and applying both primary and secondary methods has been transformative. It's helped me make decisions based on data rather than guesswork, from developing new products to choosing marketing channels. Market research has become an integral part of my business strategy, ensuring that every move we make is aligned with our customers' needs and market opportunities.

Defining Your Target Audience

Understanding who you're selling to is like setting the destination on your business's GPS. Without knowing your target market, you're just driving around hoping to stumble upon success. This realization hit me hard a couple of years into running my business when I noticed our marketing efforts were like shouting into a void. We were trying to appeal to everyone and ended up resonating with no one. That's when I dove deep into the concept of a target market and its critical importance.

A target market is a specific group of people most likely to buy your product or service. It's not just about who can use what you're selling but who will most likely seek it out. Identifying this group makes your marketing efforts more focused and effective. Defining our target market meant looking hard at who was already buying from us and who we wanted to serve. We considered factors like age, location, income level, and interests. But we didn't stop there.

To get even more specific, we developed an ideal customer profile. This involved creating a detailed description of a fictional person who represents our perfect customer. We gave them a name, a job, a family situation, and even hobbies. This exercise helped us visualize who we were talking to in our marketing messages, making those messages more personal and compelling.

However, identifying our target market wasn't just about demographics like age and income. We also investigated psychographics, which are the more personal characteristics of a person, including values, attitudes, interests, and lifestyle. Understanding these deeper aspects of our ideal customers' lives helped us craft marketing messages that directly addressed their desires and pain points.

Behavioristics played a big role, too. This means understanding the buying behavior of our target market, such as how often they purchase products like ours, their preferred shopping channels, and the factors that influence their buying decisions. For instance, we found that a significant portion of our target market values sustainability and prefers to shop online. This insight led us to highlight our eco-friendly practices more prominently and improve our online shopping experience.

Combining demographics, psychographics, and behavioristics could segment our market into more specific niches. This segmentation allowed us to tailor our products, messaging, and marketing strategies to meet different groups' unique needs and preferences within our broader target market.

In the end, defining our target audience transformed our business. Our marketing became more efficient, product development more focused, and customer satisfaction rates soared. Moving from a one-size-fits-all approach to a targeted strategy that acknowledges our customer base's diverse needs and desires was a game-changer.

ANALYZING THE COMPETITION

Understanding your competition is like knowing the other players in a game. It's not about copying them or worrying about every move they make. Instead, it's about seeing where you fit in the landscape and how to stand out. When I realized this, it changed how I approached my business strategy.

Competitive analysis is all about getting a clear picture of your market and the other businesses you're up against. It's crucial because it helps you understand what's already out there, what's working, and where there might be gaps you can fill. For me, conducting a competitive analysis meant looking at other businesses in my field to see what they were offering, how they were marketing themselves, and what customers were saying about them.

There are a few techniques I found helpful for this. First, I started with online research, looking at competitors' websites, social media profiles, and customer reviews. This gave me a good sense of their public image and how they interact with customers. Then, I looked at their product offerings and pricing to see how mine compared. I also signed up for their newsletters and followed them on social media to keep tabs on their marketing efforts and promotions.

However, the most valuable insights came from talking to customers and listening to what they liked and didn't like about my competitors. This could be through surveys, informal conversations, or social media interactions. Customers are usually more than willing to share their opinions; this feedback was gold. It showed me where my competitors were strong and where they were falling short.

Learning from competitors' strengths and weaknesses allowed me to adjust my business strategy. For example, if I noticed a competitor was strong in customer service, it pushed me to up my game in that area. On the other hand, if customers were complaining about a lack of product variety from another business, I saw an opportunity to differentiate my offerings.

In the end, analyzing the competition wasn't about beating them at their own game. It was about finding my unique space in the market and filling needs that were currently unmet. It helped me to focus not on competing on price or copying what others were doing but on building a brand that stood out for its unique strengths and values.

UNDERSTANDING MARKET TRENDS

Market trends can significantly impact your business strategy. They can change how customers think about your products or services, influence consumer behavior, and even shift the entire direction of your industry. I learned early on that being adaptable and responsive to these changes could make all the difference.

I've developed a few habits to stay informed about industry changes and consumer behavior shifts. First, I make it a point to read industry news and reports regularly. This helps me keep a pulse on what's happening and what experts predict for the future. I also attend trade shows and networking events where I can talk to peers and get insights into emerging trends.

Social media and online forums have been invaluable tools as well. They offer a direct line to what consumers are talking about and what they're interested in. By paying attention to these conversations, I've been able to anticipate changes in consumer preferences and adjust my offerings accordingly.

Adapting to market trends is more than a survival tactic; it's an opportunity to innovate and differentiate your business. For example, when I noticed a growing trend toward sustainability in my industry, I saw an opportunity to incorporate eco-friendly practices into my operations and marketing. This helped reduce my environmental impact and appealed to a segment of consumers who valued sustainability, giving me a competitive edge.

Another trend I adapted to was the increasing importance of online presence. As more consumers started shopping online, I invested in improving my website and e-commerce capabilities. This helped me reach a wider audience and provided a better shopping experience for my customers, which led to increased loyalty and sales.

Understanding and adapting to market trends is essential for any business looking to stay relevant and competitive. It requires staying informed, being flexible, and sometimes taking risks to innovate.

LEVERAGING MARKET INSIGHTS

Translating market research into actionable business strategies starts with deep diving into the data and trends you've gathered. It's about looking beyond the numbers and seeing the story they tell about your customers' needs, preferences, and behaviors. For instance, when I noticed a trend in my market research indicating a growing demand for sustainable products,

I didn't just see it as a passing interest. I saw it as a clear direction for where to take my product line next. This insight led me to source more eco-friendly materials and highlight these features in my marketing, which resonated well with my target audience and set my business apart from competitors.

Tailoring products, services, and marketing messages to meet market needs is all about alignment. It's ensuring that what you offer matches what your customers are looking for. This could mean tweaking your product design, adding new features, or changing your messaging to speak directly to your audience's desires and pain points. For example, after realizing that convenience was a top priority for my customers, I introduced a subscription service that delivered my products directly to their door. This addressed their need for convenience and built customer loyalty and recurring revenue for my business.

However, leveraging market insights isn't a one-time task; it's an ongoing process. Markets evolve, trends shift, and customer preferences change. That's why I continuously gather and analyze market data, keeping my finger on the pulse of my industry. This proactive approach has allowed me to stay ahead of changes, adapt my strategies, and continue meeting my customers' needs effectively.

Leveraging market insights is crucial for any business looking to thrive in today's competitive landscape. It's about turning data into decisions, aligning your offerings with market needs, and staying adaptable to change. By doing so, you can navigate your business journey with confidence, knowing that a deep understanding of your market informs every step you take.

Engaging with Your Market

Building a strong presence within your target market starts with visibility. You need to be where your customers are, whether that's online, in local communities, or at industry events. I made it a point to increase my business's presence on social media platforms where I knew my customers spent their time. By sharing useful content, responding to comments, and participating in conversations, I built a recognizable and trusted brand within my market.

The importance of customer feedback cannot be overstated. It's like having a compass that guides your business decisions. Gathering feedback effectively means making it easy for customers to share their thoughts with you through surveys, your website feedback forms, or direct conversations. I regularly ask for feedback through email surveys and make sure to act on what I learn. For example, when customers expressed a desire for more eco-friendly packaging, I took steps to source sustainable materials and communicated these changes back to my customers, showing them that their feedback directly influenced our practices.

Developing a continuous dialogue with your market is about more than just transactional interactions. It's about creating a community around your brand where customers feel heard, valued, and connected. I've found that regular updates about our business, behind-the-scenes looks at our operations, and stories about how we're addressing customer needs help to keep the conversation going. Additionally, hosting online Q&A sessions and being active in relevant online forums have been great ways to foster loyalty and trust. This ongoing dialogue has helped retain customers and turn them into advocates for our brand.

In essence, engaging with your market is about showing up consistently, listening actively, and responding authentically. It's a commitment to understanding and meeting your customers' needs, not just once but as an ongoing part of your business strategy. Doing so can build a loyal customer base that supports your business and contributes to its growth and success.

CHALLENGES IN UNDERSTANDING YOUR MARKET

Understanding your market is crucial, but it's not always a walk in the park. There are plenty of hurdles along the way, from figuring out who your customers are to keeping up with their ever-changing needs and preferences. I've faced my fair share of these challenges, and I've learned that overcoming them requires a mix of persistence, creativity, and a willingness to learn.

One of the biggest obstacles is getting accurate and relevant data. When I first tried to understand my market, I found myself drowning in information, not all of which was useful. It was like trying to find a needle in a haystack. I quickly learned that not all data is created equal, and the key is to focus on sources directly relevant to my business and customers. I started using targeted surveys and social media analytics to get insights directly from my audience, which proved to be much more effective than broad market reports.

Another challenge is staying ahead of market trends. The market can shift rapidly, and what worked yesterday might not work tomorrow. To keep up, I've made it a habit to continuously monitor industry news, participate in online forums, and attend trade shows. This proactive approach has helped me anticipate changes and adapt my strategies accordingly. For instance, when I noticed a growing demand for sustainable products in my industry, I was quick to explore eco-friendly options, which have since become a key selling point for my business.

Overcoming these challenges hasn't been easy, but it has been possible through innovative approaches and a commitment to understanding my customers. I've used social media not just for marketing but as a tool for engaging directly with my audience, asking them what they want and how I can serve them better. I've also invested in customer relationship management (CRM) software to track customer interactions and feedback, which has been invaluable in tailoring my offerings to meet their needs.

Understanding your market is an ongoing process that involves navigating through a lot of noise to get valuable insights. It requires being open to new technologies and methods for gathering and analyzing data and being adaptable to the insights you uncover. The challenges are real, but with a strategic approach and a bit of creativity, they can be overcome, paving the way for deeper market understanding and business growth.

TOOLS AND RESOURCES

Navigating the world of market research can feel like setting sail on vast, uncharted waters for many business owners, myself included. When I first dipped my toes into understanding my market, I quickly realized the importance of having the right tools and resources at my disposal. It wasn't just about gathering data; it was about gathering the right kind of data and then knowing what to do with it.

Digital tools have been a game-changer in this journey. For example, online surveys and social media analytics platforms have allowed me to tap directly into my audience's thoughts and preferences. These tools have made it possible to collect feedback in real-time, which is invaluable. Then there's Google Analytics, which has been like a compass, guiding me through website traffic patterns to understand where my visitors come from and what they're looking for.

However, tools are just one part of the equation. Educating myself on using these tools effectively and interpreting the data they provide has been equally important. I've turned to various resources to sharpen my skills, from online courses offered by marketing experts to webinars and eBooks. Websites like HubSpot and Moz have been treasure troves of information, offering in-depth guides on everything from SEO to content marketing strategies that attract and engage the right audience.

I also recommend keeping up with industry blogs and joining online forums where fellow entrepreneurs share insights and experiences. These communities have been invaluable for learning practical tips and staying updated on the latest market research trends.

Understanding your market in today's digital age means being both a navigator and a learner. It's about leveraging the best digital tools to gather data and committing to continuous education to make sense of that data. The journey doesn't end with finding the right information; it's an ongoing process of adaptation and learning. For anyone looking to deepen their market understanding, embracing these digital tools and resources is not just beneficial; it's essential for staying competitive and responsive to your audience's needs.

Understanding your market is not just a task to check off when setting up your business; it's a crucial part of your journey toward success. It guides your decisions, from the products or services you offer to how you communicate with your customers. My journey has taught me that the more you know about your market, the better equipped you are to meet its needs and, ultimately, to grow your business.

I want to encourage every business owner to see market understanding not as a chore but as an investment. It's an investment in your business's future and your growth as an entrepreneur. The time and resources you dedicate to understanding your market today will pay dividends down the line. It's about laying a foundation that your business can build upon, one that allows you to adapt and thrive no matter what challenges come your way.

Markets are living, breathing entities. They change and evolve, influenced by countless factors, from technological advancements to shifts in consumer behavior. Staying engaged with your market means staying relevant. It means being able to anticipate changes and pivot your strategies accordingly. This dynamic nature of markets makes business exciting and, at times, challenging. However, it also creates opportunities for those willing to listen, learn, and adapt.

As we wrap up this chapter, I hope you're feeling motivated to dive deeper into understanding your market. Remember, this is not a one-time effort but a continuous process. The landscape will shift, new competitors will emerge, and customer preferences will evolve. Your ability to engage with these changes, learn from them, and use them to inform your business strategies will set you apart. Keep your finger on the pulse of your market, stay curious, and never stop learning. The success of your business depends on it.

4

ACQUISITION CHANNELS AND SALES TACTICS

Diversifying isn't just a buzzword; it's a survival strategy in today's competitive market. I learned the hard way that relying on a single channel was like walking a tightrope without a safety net. It was a risky move that could have cost me my business. By focusing on one platform, I was missing out on a whole spectrum of opportunities to connect with potential clients who hung out in different places or responded better to other types of engagement.

This realization led me to explore and invest in various channels—email marketing, SEO, PPC, and even old-school networking events. Each channel opened new doors and brought in clients I would have never reached otherwise. It was like fishing in multiple ponds instead of stubbornly waiting for a catch in a puddle. This shift didn't just increase my client base; it transformed my business's resilience, making it less vulnerable to changes in market trends or platform algorithms.

This chapter is about that journey and the lessons learned along the way. It's a guide to not just surviving but thriving by tapping into the power of multiple acquisition channels and sales tactics. Whether you're a seasoned entrepreneur or just starting out, understanding the importance of diversification will be a game-changer for your business.

Understanding Acquisition Channels

Acquisition channels are the pathways through which we introduce our business to potential clients and guide them toward making a purchase. Think of them as the various doors and windows through which customers can enter our store in the vast mall of the market. These channels are crucial because they're how we reach out and connect with our audience, wherever they may be spending their time.

There's a whole world of channels out there, each with its unique strengths and audience. Digital channels, like social media, email marketing, and SEO, are powerful tools for reaching a broad audience relatively cheaply. Traditional channels, such as print ads, billboards, and TV commercials, still hold sway in capturing the attention of a demographic that values tangible, offline experiences. Then, there are direct channels, which involve reaching out to potential customers personally, perhaps through direct mail or face-to-face meetings at trade shows. Indirect channels might include leveraging partnerships with other businesses to tap into their customer base.

Choosing the right channels for your business isn't about throwing darts in the dark and hoping something sticks. It's about knowing your audience inside and out. Who are they? Where do they hang out? What kind of messaging resonates with them? Answering these questions can help you narrow down which channels will most likely reach your target customers effectively.

For instance, if your business targets young professionals, you might find more success with digital channels like LinkedIn or targeted PPC campaigns on search engines. On the other hand, if your market is more local and community-based, traditional advertising in local newspapers or community events might bring better results.

In my journey, I learned not just to pick channels based on trends or gut feelings but to make informed decisions based on my audience's behaviors and preferences. It involved a lot of trial and error and paying close attention to metrics and feedback to understand which channels were truly delivering value and which were not. This approach helped me allocate my resources more effectively, ensuring that I invested in channels that mattered to my business's growth.

DIGITAL ACQUISITION CHANNELS

In today's digital age, mastering online acquisition channels is not just an option; it's necessary for any business looking to thrive. Let me walk you through some digital channels that have been game-changers for my business.

First is Search Engine Optimization, or SEO. This is all about making your website more visible on search engines like Google. When someone searches for a product or service you offer, you want your site to be one of the first they see. SEO involves optimizing your website's content and structure to rank higher in search results. It's a long game, requiring patience and consistent effort, but the payoff is huge. Organic reach means reaching potential customers without directly paying for ads. It builds credibility and trust with your audience.

Then there's Pay-Per-Click (PPC) advertising. Unlike SEO, PPC offers immediate results. You create ads and bid on keywords related to your business. Every time someone clicks on your ad, you pay a fee. The beauty of PPC is its ability to target specific demographics, interests, and even behaviors. It's like using a sniper rifle instead of a shotgun to reach your target market. While it does cost money, the ability to target potential customers precisely makes it incredibly efficient.

Social media platforms are another cornerstone of digital acquisition. Platforms like Facebook, Instagram, and LinkedIn offer unique opportunities to engage with your audience. It's not just about posting ads; it's about creating content that resonates with your followers, encourages interaction, and builds a community around your brand. Each platform has its strengths and caters to different audiences, so understanding where your customers spend their time is key. Social media is also great for driving traffic to your website and converting followers into customers.

Last, there's email marketing. Some say email is dead, but they couldn't be more wrong. Email marketing remains one of the most effective ways to nurture leads and convert prospects into loyal customers. It allows for personalized communication, offering value through newsletters, exclusive deals, and insightful content. The key is to provide relevant and valuable content, turning subscribers into engaged customers.

Incorporating these digital channels into my business strategy wasn't easy. It took a lot of learning, tweaking, and sometimes starting from scratch. But by focusing on these areas, I was able to significantly increase my reach, engage more deeply with my customers, and drive conversions. The digital landscape is always changing, so staying adaptable and continuously optimizing your strategies is crucial.

Traditional Acquisition Channels

While the digital realm offers vast opportunities, I've learned not to underestimate the power and personal touch of more traditional methods.

Networking and community involvement have been invaluable. Getting out there, shaking hands, and making personal connections can make all the difference. It's about more than just selling; it's about building relationships that can lead to lasting business opportunities. Whether sponsoring a local sports team or participating in community service, these activities put a face to your business and embed you within the local fabric.

Print advertising still holds its ground, especially for reaching certain demographics. For instance, local newspapers and specialized magazines can be gold mines for targeting an audience that prefers tangible reading material. It's about knowing your audience and where they spend their time. Crafting messages that resonate with them through these mediums can drive surprising results.

Direct mail campaigns have evolved but are far from obsolete. In an age where inboxes are cluttered with digital marketing, a well-designed, tangible piece of mail can stand out. The key is personalization and relevance. Tailoring your message to the recipient, offering genuine value, and making it visually appealing can reinvigorate this traditional channel and yield high engagement.

Trade shows and events offer a unique opportunity for direct engagement. Something about face-to-face interaction builds trust in a way digital channels can't replicate. Demonstrating your product, answering questions in real time, and receiving immediate feedback are invaluable. These events are a hotbed for networking, not just with potential clients but with peers who can offer insights, partnerships, and growth opportunities.

Incorporating these traditional channels into my business strategy has taught me the importance of balance. While it's crucial to keep up with digital trends, a whole spectrum of opportunities in the traditional realm can complement and enhance your overall acquisition strategy. It's about blending the old with the new to create a comprehensive approach that reaches your audience wherever they may be.

SALES TACTICS FOR CONVERSION

Understanding the sales funnel and the customer journey has been a game-changer for my business. It's about recognizing that not every potential customer is ready to buy the moment they learn about your product or service. Some are just discovering their needs, while others are comparing options or ready to make a purchase. Tailoring our approach to each stage of this journey has helped us more effectively guide prospects toward making a decision.

Effective communication is at the heart of sales success. It's not just about talking; it's about listening to what the customer needs and responding in a way that shows you understand and can provide a solution. This skill has helped me and my team build stronger relationships with our clients, making them feel heard and valued. It's about creating a connection that goes beyond the transaction.

Overcoming objections is another critical aspect. Every sales conversation will have its hurdles, but learning to anticipate and address these objections has helped us turn skepticism into confidence. It's about being prepared, understanding common concerns, and having clear, honest responses that alleviate doubts. This approach helps close deals and builds trust, showing that we're not just here to sell but to solve a problem.

Creating a sense of urgency and leveraging scarcity has also been effective. This doesn't mean pressuring customers but highlighting the value of what we offer and the benefits of acting now. Whether it's a limited-time offer, exclusive access, or highlighting the cost of inaction, these tactics encourage prospects to move forward. It's about making them see what they might miss out on, not through fear, but by emphasizing the positive outcomes of their decision.

Incorporating these sales tactics into our strategy has improved our conversion rates and deepened our understanding of our customers. It's a continuous learning process, adapting and refining our approach as we gain more insights into our market and what drives our customers to make a purchase. This journey has taught me that sales is not just about selling but about building relationships, understanding needs, and providing value every step of the way.

BUILDING AND TRAINING A SALES TEAM

Building and training a sales team has been one of the most critical steps in the growth of my business. It's about finding individuals who not only have the skills to sell but also share the vision and values of the company. When hiring for sales, I look for qualities like resilience, excellent communication skills, and a genuine desire to help customers. These traits often predict success in a sales role more accurately than just experience.

Once the right team is in place, training and development become the foundation of their effectiveness. We've implemented a comprehensive training program that covers product knowledge, understanding our customers' needs, and mastering sales techniques. But it doesn't stop there. Ongoing development opportunities are crucial for keeping the team sharp and up to date with the latest trends and strategies.

Motivation and incentives are also key to driving performance. Recognizing achievements through financial rewards, career advancement opportunities, or public acknowledgment has been vital. It's about creating an environment where success is celebrated, and everyone is driven to achieve their best.

Setting and monitoring key performance indicators (KPIs) for sales success has helped us stay on track and identify areas for improvement. These metrics give us a clear picture of where we excel and where we need to adjust our strategies. They're not just numbers but insights into how effectively we're meeting our customers' needs and achieving our business goals.

Building a successful sales team is an ongoing process of hiring the right people, providing them with the tools they need to succeed, motivating them to achieve their best, and using data to guide our strategies. It's a challenging journey, but one that's essential for the growth and success of the business.

Leveraging Technology in Sales

In today's fast-paced market, leveraging technology in sales isn't just an option; it's a necessity. It was a game-changer when I integrated Customer Relationship Management (CRM) systems into our sales process. These systems allowed us to manage customer relationships and sales pipelines more efficiently. Suddenly, we had a clear view of every customer's journey, from initial contact to purchase and beyond. This visibility enabled us to tailor our interactions and ensure no opportunity slipped through the cracks.

Automation tools have also been instrumental in streamlining our sales processes and enhancing customer engagement. By automating routine tasks, we've been able to focus more on building relationships and less on administrative work. Whether scheduling follow-ups or sending personalized emails, automation has helped us maintain a high level of service without increasing our workload.

Perhaps the most significant impact has come from using analytics and data-driven decision-making. Sales strategies that used to be based on gut feelings or assumptions are now grounded in solid data. We analyze everything from customer behavior patterns to sales conversion rates, using this information to refine our approach and make informed decisions about where to focus our efforts.

Integrating technology into our sales process has not only made us more efficient but also more effective. CRM systems, automation tools, and analytics have allowed us to understand our customers better, anticipate their needs, and deliver the right message at the right time. It's a powerful combination has driven our success and will continue to be a cornerstone of our sales strategy.

Refining and Optimizing Sales Strategies

In the world of business, staying still means falling behind. That's why refining and optimizing our sales strategies has become a routine part of our operations. Continuous improvement is necessary to stay competitive and meet our customers' evolving needs.

One of the key ways we've managed to keep our sales strategies sharp is through relentless feedback and analytics. After every campaign, we dive into the data, looking at what worked, what didn't, and why. This isn't always easy. Sometimes, it means acknowledging that a strategy we were excited about fell flat. But every piece of data is a chance to learn and get better.

Adapting our sales tactics based on this feedback and the ever-changing market landscape has been crucial. For instance, when we noticed a shift in how our customers preferred to be contacted, we adjusted our approach immediately. Instead of sticking to our old methods, we embraced new channels our customers were more responsive to. This agility has been key to our growth. It's about listening to the market and our customers and then being willing to pivot when necessary.

This process of refinement and optimization is ongoing. The market never stands still, and neither do our customers' needs. By staying flexible and responsive, we've been able to navigate changes that would have otherwise caught us off guard. It's a continuous cycle of learning, adapting, and improving, and it's what keeps us moving forward.

As we wrap up this chapter, it's crucial to remember the core message: the power of a multi-channel approach and dynamic sales tactics in the journey of business growth. This isn't just about spreading our efforts across various platforms or trying out every new sales technique that comes our way. It's about understanding our customers deeply, recognizing where they are, and meeting them there with solutions that resonate.

From the beginning, my journey has taught me that sticking to a single method of reaching out to potential clients or relying on outdated sales tactics is a surefire way to stagnate. The business landscape is ever evolving, and so are the needs and behaviors of our customers. Embracing a variety of acquisition channels and being agile in our sales approach has not just been beneficial; it's been essential.

I want to encourage every reader not to shy away from experimentation. The fear of failure can be a significant barrier, but it's through trying new strategies, measuring their impact, and refining our approach that we find what truly works for our unique businesses. This experimentation, measurement, and refinement cycle is the heartbeat of sustained growth. It keeps us relevant, competitive, and aligned with our customers' needs.

Never underestimate the power of well-thought-out acquisition channels and sales tactics. They are not just tools in our arsenal but the foundation upon which successful businesses are built. As you progress, keep pushing the boundaries, stay curious, and remain committed to learning and adapting. The path to business success is a marathon, not a sprint; those who are willing to evolve continuously will cross the finish line.

5

THE ROLE OF TECHNOLOGY
AND CONTENT

When I first heard about all the digital tools and content marketing strategies out there, I was skeptical. My business was doing fine with the traditional methods we'd used for years. Why fix something that wasn't broken? However, as I watched the market evolve and saw how competitors leveraged technology to get ahead, I realized I risked being left behind.

It wasn't an overnight change. At first, the world of digital marketing and technology seemed overwhelming. There were so many tools and platforms, each promising to revolutionize my business. Where was I even supposed to start? But I knew that to stay relevant and continue to grow, I needed to adapt. So, I took the plunge.

I started small, with a basic website and a social media account. It was a learning curve, figuring out how to create content that resonated with my audience and how to use these platforms to truly engage with customers. But as I got more comfortable, I began to see the power of these digital tools. They allowed me to reach a wider audience, engage with customers on a new level, and streamline operations in ways I hadn't imagined.

The real turning point came when I launched our first content marketing campaign. It was a series of blog posts designed to help customers solve common problems related to our products. The response was incredible. Not only did our website traffic increase, but customers began to see us as experts in our field. They were coming to us not just for our products but for advice and information.

This journey from skepticism to embracing digital transformation taught me a valuable lesson. Technology and content aren't just about keeping up with trends; they're about connecting with customers in meaningful ways and building a stronger, more resilient business. Now, I can't imagine running my business without them.

EMBRACING DIGITAL TRANSFORMATION

Embracing digital transformation wasn't just a choice; it became a necessity for my business. At first, integrating new technology into every aspect of operations seemed daunting. I was used to doing things a certain way, and the thought of learning all these new tools and changing established processes was overwhelming. However, I knew that to stay competitive and meet the evolving needs of my customers, I had to make a change.

The journey into digital transformation began with identifying areas within my business that could benefit most from technology. Customer engagement was the first on my list. I started using social media platforms not just to post updates but to engage with customers, answer their questions, and gather feedback. It was a game-changer. Suddenly, I was having real conversations with my customers, learning about their needs and preferences in a way I never had before.

Next, I explored digital tools for data analysis. Implementing analytics tools on our website and social media accounts allowed me to understand which content was resonating with our audience and why. This insight was invaluable. It helped me make informed decisions about our marketing strategies, leading to more effective campaigns and better use of our budget.

Operational efficiency was another area where digital tools made a significant impact. From inventory management to scheduling, there were tools available that could automate tasks, reduce errors, and save time. Implementing these tools wasn't always easy, and my team and I had a learning curve. But the benefits were undeniable. We could do more with less, freeing time to focus on growth and innovation.

The necessity of integrating technology into my business operations became clear as I saw the tangible benefits it brought. Efficiency improved, customer engagement deepened, and we could scale our operations in ways I hadn't imagined possible. Digital transformation was no longer a buzzword but a reality propelling my business forward.

THE POWER OF CONTENT MARKETING

Content marketing is the art of communicating with your customers and prospects without directly selling to them. Instead of pitching your products or services, you provide information that makes your buyer more intelligent. The essence of this content strategy is the belief that if businesses deliver consistent, ongoing, valuable information to buyers, they ultimately reward us with their business and loyalty.

Developing a compelling content marketing plan began with understanding our audience deeply. We needed to know who they were, what they cared about, their challenges, and how our products or services fit into their lives. This understanding became the foundation of our content strategy. We aimed to create content that answered their questions, provided solutions, and entertained them while subtly aligning with our business goals.

Our strategy included a mix of blog posts, videos, infographics, and social media content. Each piece of content was crafted with a specific goal: to drive traffic to our website, increase product awareness, or establish thought leadership in our industry. We focused on creating high-quality, relevant content that our audience would find valuable and shareable.

The impact of our content marketing efforts was profound. Not only did we see an increase in website traffic and engagement, but we also built a stronger, more loyal customer base. Our content helped position our brand as a trusted authority in our field, leading to more sales and higher customer retention rates.

Content marketing became the heartbeat of our digital marketing strategy. It allowed us to genuinely connect with our audience, providing them with valuable information that helped solve their problems. This approach helped us achieve our business goals and created a community of engaged customers who believed in our brand.

DIGITAL TOOLS FOR BUSINESS GROWTH

When I first integrated digital tools into my business operations, it felt like unlocking a new level of growth and understanding of my market. Customer Relationship Management (CRM) systems, analytics, and automation tools stood out as game-changers among these tools.

CRM systems transformed how we interacted with customers and managed sales processes. Suddenly, every customer interaction became an opportunity to learn and improve. We could track customer behaviors, preferences, and feedback, which allowed us to tailor our approach to meet their needs more effectively. It wasn't just about managing customer information but building relationships. By understanding our customers better, we could serve them more personally and efficiently, increasing satisfaction and loyalty.

Then, there were the analytics and data visualization tools. These tools shed light on the vast amounts of data we collected, turning it into actionable insights. We could see which products were in demand, identify market trends, and understand our customer demographics better. This information was invaluable. It informed our decision-making process, from marketing strategies to product development, ensuring that we stayed ahead of the curve and aligned with our customers' evolving needs.

Automation tools were the final piece of the puzzle. They allowed us to streamline our marketing, sales, and customer service processes, significantly increasing efficiency. Tasks that once took hours, like sending out marketing emails or updating sales records, were automated, freeing our team to focus on more strategic activities. This improved our productivity and ensured that we could maintain a high level of service as our business grew.

Integrating these digital tools into our business wasn't just about adopting new technologies but about embracing a new way of working. It made us more agile, informed, and connected to our customers. The impact on our business was profound, leading to growth that we couldn't have achieved otherwise. It was a clear reminder that leveraging the right tools can be the difference between staying stagnant and scaling new heights in today's digital age.

BUILDING AN ONLINE PRESENCE

Building a strong online presence has become a cornerstone of success in today's digital world. For my business, establishing a cohesive digital footprint across our website, social media platforms, and online marketplaces wasn't just about being visible; it was about connecting with our customers where they spent most of their time.

The journey to enhance our online presence began with our website. It's the digital storefront for any business, and for us, it was crucial that ours not only looked professional but also provided a seamless user experience. We focused on clear navigation, fast loading times, and mobile responsiveness, ensuring that our customers could find what they needed, regardless of their device.

Social media was another critical component. It allowed us to engage directly with our customers, share valuable content, and build a community around our brand. Each platform served a different purpose. On Instagram, we showcased our products through high-quality images and stories. LinkedIn helped us connect with other businesses and professionals. Through Facebook, we shared updates and customer stories and engaged in conversations. The key was consistent messaging and visuals across all platforms, reinforcing our brand identity.

Online marketplaces opened new avenues for us to reach customers. By listing our products on platforms where our target audience shopped, we could tap into existing traffic and gain visibility among potential customers who might not have found us otherwise. Optimizing our listings with detailed descriptions, keywords, and high-quality images was crucial in standing out in a crowded marketplace.

However, having a digital presence isn't just about setting up shop on various platforms; it's about optimizing your content to improve visibility. We invested time in understanding SEO best practices, from keyword research to meta descriptions, to ensure our website and content ranked well in search engine results. This helped attract more visitors to our site and increased our credibility and authority in our industry.

Building a strong online presence is an ongoing process that requires attention, creativity, and adaptability. It's about showing up where your customers are, providing value, and creating connections that go beyond transactions. For my business, this digital journey has attracted more customers and fostered an invaluable sense of community and loyalty.

CONTENT CREATION AND DISTRIBUTION

When it comes to content creation and distribution, understanding what truly resonates with your target audience is key. For my business, this meant diving deep into who our customers are, what they care about, and how they consume content. It wasn't about guessing or following the latest trends blindly; it was about connecting with our audience on a level that mattered to them.

Identifying the right types of content started with listening. We paid attention to our customers' questions, the problems they faced, and the conversations happening in our industry. This insight guided our content strategy, helping us decide whether to create blog posts, videos, infographics, or podcasts. Each type of content served a different purpose and appealed to different segments of our audience. For example, how-to videos were a hit for those who preferred visual learning, while in-depth articles satisfied those craving detailed information.

Creating content was just one part of the equation. Publishing and promoting it across various platforms was where the real challenge lay. We learned that consistency was crucial, not just in the frequency of our posts but in our brand voice and messaging. Whether it was a tweet, a blog post, or a YouTube video, our content had to be unmistakably us.

Promotion was strategic. We didn't just blast our content everywhere and hope for the best. We chose platforms where our audience was most active and engaged. Social media ads, email newsletters, and partnerships with influencers in our niche were all part of our promotion mix. Each piece of content had a clear call to action: sign up for our newsletter, download a guide, or simply leave a comment.

The process of creating and distributing content was a learning curve. It involved a lot of trial and error, analyzing what worked and what didn't, and being willing to pivot our strategy when necessary. But the effort was worth it. Our content attracted new customers and built trust and loyalty with our existing ones. It turned our brand into a resource, a place where people could find value whether or not they made a purchase. And that's what sets a business apart in today's digital age.

LEVERAGING SOCIAL MEDIA

Social media has become indispensable for connecting with customers and building a community around our brand. When I first dipped my toes into social media for business, I realized it was more than just posting product photos or sales announcements. It was about creating conversations, sharing valuable content, and engaging with those who supported us.

One strategy that transformed our approach was focusing on building a community. This meant asking questions, responding to comments, and sharing behind-the-scenes glimpses of our business. We wanted our followers to feel like they were part of our journey, not just spectators. For example, when we launched a new product, we didn't just announce it; we shared the story behind it, why we created it, and even involved our followers in naming it. This approach turned our social media pages into lively forums where customers felt heard and valued.

Another game-changer was using social media analytics. Initially, I was overwhelmed by the data, but once I started to dive into it, I realized how powerful it could be. Analytics showed us which posts our audience loved, the best times to post, and what kind of content led to the most website visits. This information was gold. It allowed us to refine our content strategy, focusing more on what worked and less on what didn't. For instance, our how-to videos had higher engagement rates and led to more direct inquiries about our products. So, we started producing more video content, significantly improving our overall engagement.

Leveraging social media effectively meant being willing to listen, adapt, and engage in genuine conversations. It wasn't just about broadcasting our message but about creating a space where our customers could interact with us and each other. The insights gained from analytics helped us make informed decisions, ensuring that our social media efforts contributed to building a strong, engaged community around our brand. This approach improved our relationship with existing customers and attracted new ones, proving that social media, when used thoughtfully, can be a powerful tool for business growth.

THE ROLE OF TECHNOLOGY IN CUSTOMER EXPERIENCE

Personalization technologies have allowed us to craft individualized experiences that significantly enhance customer satisfaction and loyalty. By collecting data on customer preferences and behaviors, we can now offer recommendations, content, and offers specifically aligned with each customer's interests. For example, when customers visit our website, they are greeted with products and content that match their previous interactions with us. This level of personalization has improved our sales and strengthened our customers' connection to our brand, making them feel understood and valued.

On the other hand, mobile technologies have revolutionized how customers access our services. Recognizing the shift toward mobile usage, we optimized our website and digital content for mobile users. This meant redesigning our site to ensure it was responsive, fast-loading, and easy to navigate on a smartphone or tablet. We also developed a mobile app that allowed customers to shop, access their accounts, and receive notifications about new products and promotions directly on their phones. This focus on mobile accessibility has made it incredibly convenient for our customers to interact with us, leading to increased engagement and sales.

Integrating personalization and mobile technologies into our customer experience strategy has been a game-changer. It's not just about selling products anymore; it's about creating a seamless, enjoyable experience for our customers, no matter where they are or what device they use. By leveraging these technologies, we've met our customers' expectations for personalized, accessible service, setting us apart in a competitive market.

CHALLENGES AND SOLUTIONS

One of the biggest challenges I've faced is figuring out how to effectively integrate new technologies into our operations without breaking the bank. There's always a new tool or platform promising to revolutionize your business, but with limited resources, making the right choice is crucial. We had to learn to prioritize our needs and focus on technologies that offered the most value for our specific goals. For instance, instead of jumping on every new trend, we focused on building a solid online presence and optimizing our website for mobile users, directly impacting our customer engagement and sales.

Another obstacle was the skill gap within our team. As we moved more of our operations online, it became apparent that not everyone was comfortable with the digital tools we were adopting. To address this, we invested in training and development, bringing in experts to teach us about digital marketing, social media, and data analysis. This helped us become more proficient and fostered a culture of continuous learning within our team.

Keeping up with technological advancements has been another ongoing challenge. The digital landscape changes so quickly that it can feel impossible to keep up. To stay relevant, we've prioritized staying informed about industry trends and consumer behaviors. We regularly attend webinars, participate in online forums, and subscribe to industry newsletters. This proactive approach has helped us anticipate changes and adapt our strategies accordingly, ensuring we remain competitive in a fast-paced market.

Overcoming these challenges hasn't been easy, but it has been incredibly rewarding. By embracing digital marketing and technology, we've reached new customers, improved our operations, and grown our business in ways we never thought possible. The key has been to approach each challenge as an opportunity to learn and improve, always keeping our ulti-mate goal in mind: to provide the best possible service to our customers.

FUTURE TRENDS

Looking ahead, I see a horizon filled with emerging technol-ogies that promise to reshape the way we do business and engage with our customers. The potential impact on business strategies and customer engagement is immense, from artificial intelligence and machine learning to augmented reality and blockchain. These technologies aren't just buzzwords but the building blocks of the next wave of business innovation.

Take artificial intelligence, for example. It's already starting to transform customer service through chatbots and personalized shopping experiences. Imagine being able to predict your customers' needs before they even articulate them, offering solutions and products tailored precisely to their preferences. That's the kind of game-changing strategy that can set a business apart in a crowded marketplace.

Augmented reality is another area ripe with potential. It could revolutionize the retail industry by allowing customers to visualize products in their homes before purchasing. This level of interaction and engagement could dramatically enhance the online shopping experience, leading to higher satisfaction and loyalty.

However, with these opportunities comes the challenge of staying ahead of the curve. The pace of technological change is faster than ever, and what's cutting-edge today may be obsolete tomorrow. Preparing for future trends requires a commitment to continuous learning and flexibility. It means keeping a close eye on industry developments, listening to customer feedback, and being willing to pivot your strategy in response to new information.

As a business owner, I'm excited about the possibilities of these emerging technologies. I'm also mindful of the need to approach them thoughtfully, ensuring that any new tools or strategies we adopt align with our core values and business goals. By staying informed, agile, and customer focused, I'm confident we can navigate the future of technology and content marketing, leveraging these advances to build deeper connections with our customers and drive our business forward.

It's clear that technology and content aren't just parts of the business landscape; they're at the heart of how we achieve success today. From how we connect with our customers to the efficiency of our operations, every aspect of our business is touched by these elements. My journey has taught me that embracing digital tools and content marketing isn't optional—it's essential for growth and staying competitive.

I remember the days when integrating technology into every facet of my business seemed daunting. It was a shift from the traditional way I was used to running things. But as I took the plunge, I saw firsthand its transformative impact—not just in streamlining operations but in deepening the connections with my customers. Content marketing opened new avenues for engagement, allowing us to share our story and values in ways that resonated deeply with our audience.

But the journey doesn't end here. The landscape of technology and content is ever evolving, and staying static means falling behind. I've learned that success lies in continually exploring new tools, adapting to changes, and innovating how we use content to speak to our customers. It's about being curious, open to change, and willing to take calculated risks.

I encourage you to view technology and content not as challenges to overcome but as opportunities to propel your business forward. Dive into understanding the digital tools at your disposal. Craft content that genuinely speaks to and engages your audience. And most importantly, keep pushing the boundaries of what's possible.

Innovation, adaptability, and a willingness to learn are your best tools in this journey. With them, you can navigate the complexities of today's business environment and thrive within it. Let's embrace the digital age and see where this exciting journey can take us.

6

CUSTOMER RETENTION AND RELATIONSHIP BUILDING

Starting a business is one thing, but keeping it running successfully is another ball game. One of the biggest lessons I've learned on this journey is the undeniable importance of holding onto your customers. It's not just about making a sale; it's about creating a bond that keeps them coming back for more. In today's fiercely competitive market, where customers have endless options at their fingertips, the ability to retain them can truly make or break your business.

Building and maintaining strong customer relationships is the backbone of business sustainability and growth. It's like nurturing a garden. You plant the seeds (your product or service), but for those plants to grow and flourish (aka for your business to thrive), you need to water them regularly and ensure they get enough sunlight. In business terms, this means consistently meeting or exceeding customer expectations and making every interaction with your brand positive and memorable.

I've seen firsthand how focusing on customer retention has propelled my business forward. It's not just about repeat sales, although those are certainly important. It's about turning satisfied customers into loyal advocates for your brand. These are the people who will sing your praises to friends and family, essentially doing your marketing for you. And there's no advertising more powerful than word-of-mouth recommendations from trusted sources.

As we dive deeper into this chapter, remember that the effort you put into keeping your customers happy is an investment in the future of your business. Strong relationships don't just contribute to business sustainability; they drive growth. They're the reason customers choose you over a competitor and the foundation upon which you can build a lasting enterprise.

The Cost of Acquisition vs. Retention

When I first grasped the concept of customer acquisition versus retention, it was eye-opening for me. It's like comparing the effort of fishing in a vast ocean to keep the fish you've already caught in your pond. Acquiring new customers is essential, sure, but it's also a costly affair. From marketing campaigns to special offers designed to lure them in, the expenses add up quickly. On the other hand, keeping the customers you already have requires a different kind of effort, one that's often more about quality service and building relationships than spending on advertising.

The numbers put things into perspective. Studies have shown that attracting a new customer can cost five times more than keeping an existing one. That's a significant difference. But here's where it gets even more interesting: Increasing your customer retention rates by just 5 percent can boost your profits by 25 percent to 95 percent. These statistics made me realize the true value of focusing on the customers I already had. It wasn't just about saving money but tapping into the potential for much greater profitability.

This understanding led me to shift my focus. Instead of pouring all our resources into chasing new customers, we invested more in the ones we already had. We explored improving our service, adding more value to our existing offerings, and making sure our customers knew they were appreciated. This approach didn't just make financial sense; it also helped us build a stronger, more loyal customer base. And as our retention rates went up, so did our profits.

UNDERSTANDING CUSTOMER NEEDS AND EXPECTATIONS

Getting to the heart of what my customers wanted wasn't just a task; it became my mission. I learned early on that understanding customer needs and expectations was the cornerstone of meeting and exceeding those expectations. It wasn't about guessing or assuming; it was about knowing. And how did I get to know? Through diligent market research and a commitment to listening to what our customers had to say.

Market research was my starting point. It wasn't about fancy tools or expensive surveys but about being present where our customers were. I engaged in social media conversations, kept an eye on online forums related to our industry, and even attended community events. This wasn't passive observation. I asked questions, sought feedback, and paid attention to the trends that were important to our customers.

However, gathering feedback was only half the battle. The real magic happened in the analysis. I poured over the feedback, looking for patterns and common themes. It was like piecing together a puzzle, each piece of feedback a clue to the bigger picture of our customers' desires and pain points. This wasn't a one-time effort but an ongoing process, a continuous loop of feedback and improvement.

This approach transformed the way we did business. It wasn't just about selling a product or service anymore; it was about solving real problems for our customers, making their lives easier, and providing value in ways they hadn't even anticipated. And the more we aligned our offerings with our customers' needs and expectations, the stronger our relationships with them grew.

Understanding customer needs and expectations through market research and feedback analysis wasn't just a strategy; it became our business's lifeline. It informed every decision, from product development to customer service, ensuring that we were always moving in the right direction—toward greater customer satisfaction and loyalty.

Personalizing the Customer Experience

Personalizing the customer experience has become a game-changer in how I run my business. It's about seeing each customer as an individual with unique needs and preferences rather than just another sale. This shift in perspective came from understanding the power of customer data and how it could be used to tailor our interactions and offerings to each customer.

I started by collecting data on customer preferences, purchase history, and feedback. This wasn't about invading privacy but about paying attention to the cues our customers were already giving us. For example, if a customer frequently purchased a particular type of product, we'd make sure to notify them when similar products were available or on sale.

One strategy that paid off was segmenting our email marketing campaigns. Instead of sending the same promotional email to our entire list, we created different versions tailored to specific interests. The response was incredible. Our open rates and engagement soared because customers felt we understood what they wanted.

I also looked at businesses outside my industry for inspiration. One standout example was a coffee shop that remembered customers' names and their usual orders. This simple act of personalization made customers feel valued and increased their loyalty. I took this lesson to heart, implementing a system where we could greet repeat customers by name and make recommendations based on their past purchases.

Another example was an online retailer that used browsing history to personalize product recommendations on their website. Seeing the success of this approach, I invested in similar technology for our online store. The result was a more engaging shopping experience that led to increased sales and customer satisfaction.

By using customer data wisely and looking to successful examples for inspiration, I've created a business that truly understands and caters to the individual needs of our customers. This has improved our customer retention rates and turned our customers into advocates for our brand.

BUILDING TRUST THROUGH TRANSPARENCY AND COMMUNICATION

Building trust with customers is the foundation of everything we do in my business. I learned early on that trust isn't given; it's earned, and one of the most powerful tools for earning it is through transparency and honest communication.

A few years back, we faced a significant delay with one of our suppliers, which meant we couldn't fulfill orders on time. Initially, I was hesitant to share the bad news with our customers, fearing it would harm our reputation. However, I realized that being upfront was the only way to maintain their trust.

We sent out an email explaining the situation in detail. We apologized and outlined the steps we were taking to resolve the issue and prevent it from happening again. The response from our customers was overwhelmingly positive. They appreciated our honesty and clear communication. Many even expressed their support and understanding, which was a relief and a clear indicator that we had made the right decision.

This experience taught me the true value of transparency in business. Whether good news or bad, we make it a point to communicate openly with our customers. We update them about new products, changes in service, or even potential issues that might affect them. This approach has helped us build a loyal customer base.

Honest communication has another benefit: It invites feedback. Being open with our customers encourages them to share their thoughts and suggestions with us. This feedback has been invaluable, helping us improve our products and services in ways we hadn't considered.

Building trust through transparency and communication has been a game-changer for my business. It's not always easy to share the not-so-good news, but I've learned that customers respect and value honesty. This approach has helped us build stronger relationships with our customers, ensuring they stick with us for the long haul.

IMPLEMENTING EFFECTIVE LOYALTY PROGRAMS

Starting a loyalty program seemed like an overwhelming task at first. I knew it could be a powerful tool for keeping our customers coming back, but I wasn't sure where to begin. After some research and a lot of brainstorming with my team, we decided to dive in and give it a shot. We wanted to create something that rewarded our customers for their loyalty and felt personal and meaningful to them.

We looked at various models of loyalty programs to see what might work best for us. Some businesses use points systems, where customers earn points for every purchase they can redeem for discounts or free products. Others offered tiered rewards, giving customers greater benefits as they reached higher spending levels. We even saw some companies offering perks like free shipping or exclusive access to new products for their most loyal customers.

After considering our options, we decided to combine a few of these ideas to create a program that would be flexible yet straightforward. Our loyalty program rewards customers with points for each purchase, but we also include special bonuses for milestones, like their first purchase anniversary or after they've spent a certain amount.

Designing the program was just the first step. We knew that for it to be successful, it had to resonate with our customers. We focused on making it easy to understand and use. We didn't want our customers to jump through hoops to earn rewards. We also communicated the benefits clearly and regularly so our customers knew exactly what they were getting and how to get it.

Launching the program was a bit nerve-wracking, but the response from our customers was incredibly positive. They loved being rewarded for their loyalty, and we saw repeat purchases increase. It was clear that the program was a way to thank our customers for their business and a powerful tool for encouraging them to keep coming back.

Over time, we've continued to tweak and improve our loyalty program based on customer feedback and business goals. To keep the program exciting and engaging, we've added new rewards and adjusted the ways customers can earn points.

Implementing an effective loyalty program has significantly influenced our customer retention strategy. It's helped us build stronger relationships with our customers and has had a noticeable impact on our repeat business. The key has been to create a program that feels valuable to our customers and to remain flexible, always looking for ways to improve and evolve the program to meet the changing needs of our market.

ENGAGING CUSTOMERS THROUGH SOCIAL MEDIA AND CONTENT

In today's digital age, engaging with customers isn't just about face-to-face interactions or the occasional email blast. It's about being where they are, which, for many, means being active on social media. I quickly realized that if we wanted to keep our customers engaged and deepen our relationships with them, we needed to have a strong presence on platforms like Facebook, Instagram, and Twitter.

At first, the idea of managing social media accounts for my business was overwhelming. I wondered what I would post and whether anyone would care. However, as I dove into it, I discovered that social media was the perfect place to showcase our brand's personality and connect with our customers more personally.

We started by sharing behind-the-scenes looks at our operations, highlighting new products, and sharing stories about our team. But we didn't stop there. We also focused on creating valuable content that our customers would find useful and interesting. This included tips related to our products, industry news, and answers to common questions we heard from our customers.

The response was incredible. Our followers began to grow; more importantly, we saw real engagement. Customers commented on our posts, shared their experiences with our products, and even tagged us in their social media content. It was clear that we were building a community around our brand.

Social media wasn't just a one-way street. It also gave us invaluable insights into what our customers liked, what they didn't, and what they wanted to see more of. This feedback loop allowed us to adjust our content strategy in real time, ensuring we always delivered value to our audience.

Creating engaging content became a key part of our strategy to retain customers and keep them interested in our brand. Whether it was a blog post, a video tutorial, or an infographic, we made sure everything we put out was relevant to our audience and reinforced why they chose us in the first place.

Social media and creating valuable content have allowed us to maintain and deepen relationships with our customers, keeping them engaged and informed. It's shown me that in the digital world, staying connected with your customers means meeting them where they are and providing them with content that enriches their experience with your brand.

Leveraging Technology for Relationship Building

In the journey of growing my business, I've learned that technology isn't just about making operations more efficient; it's a powerful ally in building and nurturing customer relationships. The right tools and software can transform how we manage these relationships, making them stronger and more personal, contrary to what some might think.

One of my first steps was investing in a Customer Relationship Management (CRM) system. This wasn't just a place to store customer information; it became the backbone of our customer engagement strategy. With the CRM, we could track every interaction, from the initial contact to post-sale follow-ups, ensuring no customer felt neglected. It allowed us to personalize our communications at scale, remembering every detail, like a customer's last purchase or preferred contact method, and making them feel valued and understood.

But where technology shone in enhancing our relationships was through automation. I know what you're thinking: How can something as impersonal as automation create personal connections? The answer lies in its application. We used automation to send birthday greetings, remind customers of appointments, or follow up after a purchase to ask for feedback. These small touches, automated but deeply personal in nature, showed our customers that we cared about them, not just as sales but as people.

Moreover, automation helped us stay consistent in our communications. It ensured we were always there, reaching out with relevant information or just a friendly hello, without overwhelming our team or customers. It was like having an extra set of hands dedicated solely to keeping our customer relationships strong and vibrant.

In embracing these technologies, we found a balance. We used data and automation to enhance our understanding and outreach while always keeping the human element at the forefront. Every automated message was crafted with care, and every piece of data collected was used to better serve and understand our customers' needs.

Leveraging technology for relationship building has been a game-changer for us. Tools like CRM systems and automation have made it possible to manage relationships at scale and deepened those connections, making each customer feel seen and valued. It's a testament to how technology, when used thoughtfully, can enhance personal connections rather than hinder them.

Training Your Team on Customer Retention Strategies

Building a team that prioritizes the customer has been one of my top priorities. It's not just about hiring the right people; it's about nurturing a culture that values customer retention as much as acquisition. This mindset shift was crucial for our business, transforming how we interact with our customers and how they perceive and engage with us.

To embed this customer-first culture, we started with comprehensive training programs. These weren't your run-of-the-mill training sessions focused solely on product knowledge or sales tactics. Instead, we dove deep into the why and how of customer retention. We explored the long-term value of a customer, not just the immediate sale. This helped the team understand that every interaction with a customer is an opportunity to build a relationship, not just close a deal.

However, understanding alone wasn't enough. We needed to incentivize our team to prioritize retention actively. Therefore, we revamped our reward system, aligning it with retention metrics. Employees who went above and beyond to keep customers satisfied and engaged were recognized and rewarded. This could be through resolving a complaint in a way that exceeded the customer's expectations or through innovative ideas that improved our overall service.

Moreover, we encouraged open communication about retention strategies within the team. This wasn't a top-down directive; everyone, from customer service reps to the sales team, was invited to share their insights and suggestions. This collaborative approach led to more effective retention strategies and fostered a sense of ownership and pride among team members. They weren't just following orders; they were active participants in shaping the company's relationship with its customers.

Training your team on customer retention strategies is about more than just sharing techniques and setting targets. It's about building a culture that sees the value in every customer interaction. It's about rewarding those who contribute to retention, encouraging innovation, and fostering a sense of community and shared purpose. This approach has improved our retention rates and made our team stronger, more cohesive, and more motivated. And in the end, that's what makes all the difference.

Measuring Success and Making Adjustments

Measuring success in customer retention isn't just about looking at the numbers; it's about understanding what those numbers mean and how they can guide us toward better strategies. In our business, we've learned that keeping a close eye on key performance indicators (KPIs) like customer retention rates, customer satisfaction scores, and repeat purchase rates gives us a clear picture of where we stand.

For us, tracking these KPIs has been a game-changer. It's not just about celebrating when the numbers go up or worrying when they dip. It's about digging into the data to understand the why behind those movements. This approach has helped us identify what works and, just as importantly, what doesn't.

However, the real magic happens when we use this data to make informed adjustments to our retention strategies. For example, if we notice a dip in our customer satisfaction scores, we don't shrug it off. We dive deep to understand the root cause. Is it a product issue? A customer service hiccup? Whatever it is, we're on it, tweaking our approach, training our team differently, or even revamping a service or product.

It's not just about fixing problems. This data-driven approach also helps us identify opportunities for innovation.

Maybe we notice a trend in customer feedback that points us toward a new feature or service. Or perhaps the data shows us that customers are particularly happy with a certain aspect of our business, something we can then double down on.

The key is to stay flexible and responsive. The market changes, customer expectations evolve, and our strategies need to keep pace. By closely monitoring our KPIs and being willing to pivot our strategies based on what the data tells us, we've been able to retain customers and deepen our relationships with them.

Overcoming Common Challenges

In the journey of building and growing a business, facing challenges with customer retention is inevitable. It's not just about attracting customers but keeping them coming back. Over the years, I've encountered my fair share of hurdles in this area. Still, each challenge has been a lesson in disguise, teaching me valuable strategies for maintaining strong customer relationships.

One of the most common obstacles we've faced is customers' evolving expectations. As the market changes and new technologies emerge, so do the needs and wants of our customers. Staying ahead of these changes requires constant vigilance and a willingness to adapt quickly. For instance, when we noticed a shift in how customers preferred to interact with our service team—moving from phone calls to messaging apps—we had to overhaul our communication channels promptly. This addressed our customers' immediate preferences and signaled to them that their comfort and convenience are our top priorities.

Another frequent challenge is recovering from service failures. No matter how much we strive for perfection, mistakes happen. What matters is how we handle them. Early on, I learned the hard way that a poorly managed mistake could lead to losing a customer forever. But, when handled correctly, it can strengthen the customer's trust in your business. We've developed a protocol for these situations that starts with immediately acknowledging the mistake, followed by a sincere apology and a swift, effective resolution. More importantly, we analyze every incident to understand its root cause, ensuring we learn from each failure and reduce the chances of it happening again.

Recovering from service failures also involves exceeding the customer's expectations. It's not just about fixing what went wrong but making up for the inconvenience caused. Whether offering a discount, a freebie, or a personal follow-up call to ensure they're satisfied with the resolution, these gestures show customers they're valued.

The key to overcoming challenges in customer retention lies in being proactive, responsive, and genuinely caring about the customer experience. It's about building a culture within your business that sees every obstacle as an opportunity to improve and every failure as a lesson. This mindset has been instrumental in navigating the ups and downs of customer retention and has ultimately helped us build a loyal customer base that feels respected and valued.

Over the years, I've seen firsthand how prioritizing customer retention has stabilized our revenue and transformed our business into a brand people trust and advocate for.

The essence of our discussion boils down to a simple truth: Businesses thrive on strong, enduring relationships with their customers. It's about seeing beyond the initial sale and valuing the ongoing dialogue with those who choose our products or services. This commitment to our customers has been a guiding star, steering us through challenges and toward opportunities for deeper connections and growth.

Every customer interaction is a golden opportunity to reinforce trust, exceed expectations, and cement a relationship that can withstand the test of time. Whether a complaint is resolved with care or a personalized thank you note, these moments are the building blocks of a loyal customer base.

I encourage you to embrace the philosophy of seeing your customers as partners in your journey. Invest in understanding them, anticipate their needs, and never miss a chance to show appreciation. Your effort to retain a customer contributes to your business's success and enriches its purpose.

7

LEVERAGING SOCIAL PROOF AND REFERRALS

Social proof is the influence that the actions and attitudes of the people around us have on our behavior. This concept isn't new, but understanding its power in the context of business opened my eyes to a whole new world of possibilities. It's like when you see a line outside a restaurant; you can't help but think the food must be good. That's social proof in action.

On the other hand, referrals have always been a cornerstone of growing any business. There's something inherently trustworthy about a recommendation from a friend or family member. It's like having a direct line to potential customers who already have a positive impression of your business before they walk through the door or visit your website. The impact of a well-structured referral program can be astounding, often leading to exponential growth that would be hard to achieve through traditional marketing alone.

I remember being hesitant to dive into these strategies. I was worried they wouldn't work for my type of business or that they would be too complicated to implement. However, I saw a dramatic shift when I started integrating social proof and referrals into my marketing efforts. Sales increased, customer loyalty strengthened, and our market presence grew stronger than I had ever imagined. This chapter of my journey taught me the undeniable value of leveraging the power of social proof and referrals. It wasn't just about attracting new customers but building a community around my brand that believed in and advocated for our products and services.

SOCIAL PROOF AS A CONCEPT

Social proof is a powerful concept that revolves around the idea that people will conform to the actions of others under the assumption that those actions reflect the correct behavior. This concept is crucial in influencing decisions, especially in the business world. Several types of social proof exist, including customer testimonials, expert endorsements, celebrity endorsements, user reviews, and social media shares. Each type serves as evidence that others have endorsed a product, service, or company, which can significantly influence potential customers' decisions.

The psychological basis of social proof lies in our natural tendency to look to others for guidance when we are uncertain about how to act or what to believe. It's rooted in the human instinct to follow the crowd, assuming there's safety and accuracy in numbers. This behavior is especially prevalent in situations where we feel out of our depth or when the correct course of action is ambiguous.

One of the most compelling real-world examples of social proof is found in online reviews and ratings. Think about the last time you wanted to try a new restaurant or buy a new product online. Chances are, you looked up reviews to see what others had to say about it. A product with hundreds of positive reviews is far more likely to be purchased than one with few or negative reviews.

Harnessing the Power of Referrals

Referrals have always been a golden ticket in business, acting as a bridge of trust between a new customer and your company. They carry a weight of credibility that's hard to achieve through any other form of marketing. When someone recommends your business to a friend or family member, it's like giving your company a seal of approval that comes with built-in trust.

Creating a successful referral program isn't just about asking your customers to recommend you to others; it's about making it worth their while. The key is providing incentives to encourage your current customers to spread the word about your services or products. This could be anything from discounts, special offers, or even access to exclusive products or services for every successful referral they make. But it's not just about the rewards. A great referral program is easy to use and share. It means having a simple process where customers can easily send referrals to their friends and track their rewards.

For my business, setting up a referral program was a game-changer. We focused on making the referral process seamless, integrating it directly into our website and customer dashboard. We also communicated the benefits clearly to our customers and their friends who would be receiving the referrals. This transparency and ease of use led to a significant increase in our customer base, all thanks to the power of word-of-mouth.

Social Proof Strategies

Social proof is a pivotal part of how businesses connect with their audience in today's digital age. It's about showing potential customers your business is trusted, valued, and used by many. Here's how I've leveraged social proof to boost my business's credibility and attract more customers.

First, customer reviews and testimonials have been a game-changer. I made it a point to ask satisfied customers to share their experiences online. Whether on our website, social media, or third-party review sites, every positive review serves as a beacon, guiding new customers our way. It's amazing how a few honest words from a happy customer can instill confidence in those on the fence.

Then, there's user-generated content. I encouraged our customers to share their experiences with our products on their social media. We created hashtags and ran contests to motivate participation. Seeing real people use and enjoy our products has helped create a sense of community and authenticity around our brand that polished marketing materials alone could never achieve.

Media mentions and expert endorsements have also played a crucial role. Whenever our business gets featured in a blog, magazine, or news outlet, we make sure to share it far and wide. The same goes for endorsements from industry experts. This kind of recognition boosts our visibility and adds a layer of credibility that attracts more discerning customers.

Lastly, influencer partnerships have opened new avenues for us. By collaborating with influencers who align with our brand values, we've been able to tap into their audiences in a genuine and organic way. These partnerships have increased our reach and provided social proof that resonates with a younger, more digitally savvy customer base.

Incorporating these strategies into my business has reinforced the importance of social proof in today's market. It's not just about telling people how great your product or service is; it's about showing them through the voices and experiences of others.

Referral Program Best Practices

Creating a referral program that works is like setting up a domino effect for your business growth. It's about making one happy customer lead to another and then another. Here's how I approached it, focusing on incentives, ease of sharing, effective tracking, and promoting the program to ensure it gains traction.

First, designing the referral program was all about finding the right incentive. It wasn't just about offering something valuable to the referrer but also ensuring the new customer felt welcomed. We settled on a dual incentive structure where both the referrer and the referee would benefit. This approach seemed to hit the right note, encouraging more customers to share their love for our products.

Making the referral process easy to share was crucial. We integrated the referral program into our app and website, where customers could simply click to share a unique referral link via social media, email, or even text. This simplicity removed barriers, making it more likely for customers to spread the word.

Tracking was the backbone of our referral program. We used a system that automatically tracked referrals through unique links, crediting referrers once a new customer made a purchase. This system made it easy to distribute rewards and provided valuable data on how the program was performing.

Promoting the referral program was an ongoing effort. We highlighted it in our newsletters, on our website, and during customer service interactions. We even created social media campaigns around it, showcasing the benefits of sharing. The key was to keep the program top of mind for our customers, reminding them of the rewards they could earn.

Monitoring and refining the program based on performance data was the final piece of the puzzle. We regularly reviewed how many new customers were coming in through referrals, which incentives were most effective, and how we could simplify the sharing process even further. This data-driven approach allowed us to continuously improve the program, making it more appealing to our customers over time.

Our referral program became a powerful tool for growth, driven by our customer's satisfaction and willingness to recommend us. It's a testament to the fact that when your customers believe in what you offer, they're your best advocates.

INTEGRATING SOCIAL PROOF INTO MARKETING

Integrating social proof into our marketing strategy transformed how we connected with potential customers. It wasn't just about telling people how great our products were; it was about showing them through the experiences of others. Here's how we did it across different platforms, making our marketing efforts more authentic and impactful.

For our advertising and promotional materials, we started featuring real customer testimonials. It was a game-changer. Instead of the usual sales pitches, our ads now had quotes from satisfied customers sharing how our product made a difference in their lives. This approach added a layer of trust and relatability you can't achieve with traditional advertising.

Our website became a showcase of customer success stories. We dedicated a section to case studies detailing how our products solved real problems for real people. These stories were not just about our products' features but about our customers' experiences. It made our website more than just a place to shop; it became a source of inspiration and reassurance for potential buyers.

Email marketing was another area where we leveraged social proof. Every newsletter we sent out included a customer spotlight segment. We shared stories of how customers used our products in their daily lives, along with photos or videos they had sent us. This made our emails more engaging and encouraged more customers to share their stories with us, creating a virtuous cycle of content.

Incorporating social proof into our marketing wasn't just a tactic; it was a shift toward more authentic communication. It allowed us to build a stronger connection with our audience, making them feel part of a community rather than just consumers. This approach not only improved our conversion rates but also deepened the loyalty of our existing customers. It's a strategy that continues to pay dividends, proving that the power of real customer experiences can never be underestimated.

Building a Culture of Referrals

Building a culture of referrals within our company became a cornerstone of our growth strategy. It wasn't just about asking our customers to recommend us to others; it was about creating an environment where referrals naturally happened because of the positive experiences we provided.

First, we focused on educating our team about the importance of referrals. We held workshops and training sessions to explain how referrals directly impacted our business's success. We discussed the psychology behind why people refer services or products to others and how we could make our service so good that customers would want to talk about it.

Encouraging and rewarding our employees for generating referrals was our next step. We introduced a referral program for our staff, offering incentives for every new customer who came to us through their recommendation. This wasn't limited to our sales team; everyone in the company, from our tech support to our product development teams, was included. It turned into a bit of a friendly competition, with leaderboards and special recognition for top referrers. This boosted our referral numbers and fostered a sense of ownership and pride among our team members.

However, the most crucial aspect was creating a customer experience that naturally encouraged referrals. We knew that no incentive could replace the genuine satisfaction of our customers. We invested in understanding our customers' needs and went above and beyond to meet them. We personalized our interactions and made sure our customers knew they were valued. We followed up on their experiences and made improvements based on their feedback.

This approach turned our customers into our biggest advocates. They started referring us not because we asked them to but because they believed in our product and wanted others to benefit from it, too. Our business grew, and so did our reputation, all because we focused on building a culture where referrals were a natural outcome of our exceptional service. It was a powerful lesson in the value of focusing on people—our team and our customers—and its incredible impact on a business.

MEASURING THE IMPACT

We knew social proof and referrals were important, but understanding their real value to our business required a deep dive into the data. We started by identifying the right tools and metrics that could give us a clear picture of their effectiveness.

For social proof, we tracked metrics like conversion rates on pages where we showcased customer testimonials versus pages without them. We also monitored the engagement rates on social media posts that included user-generated content. For our referral program, we kept a close eye on the number of new customers acquired through referrals and the overall cost of acquiring these customers compared to other channels.

We used a variety of tools to gather and analyze this data. Customer relationship management (CRM) software helped us track the source of new leads and conversions, while web analytics tools gave us insights into how users interacted with our website. Social media analytics were invaluable in understanding which types of content resonated most with our audience.

Analyzing this data opened our eyes to the ROI of our social proof and referral efforts. We could see how many new customers we were gaining through referrals and how their lifetime value compared to customers acquired through other means. This data helped us understand that customers who came to us through referrals tended to be more loyal and had a higher average purchase value.

Armed with this knowledge, we doubled down on our efforts to encourage and showcase social proof and to make our referral program even more appealing. We fine-tuned our strategies based on what the data was telling us, focusing more on what worked best and cutting back on what didn't.

This approach to measuring the impact and continuously optimizing our strategies based on data improved our marketing efficiency and significantly contributed to our bottom line. It taught us that what gets measured gets managed, and by paying close attention to the effectiveness of our social proof and referral strategies, we could make informed decisions that drove our business forward.

Overcoming Challenges

It wasn't all smooth sailing when we first started focusing on social proof and referral strategies. We faced our fair share of challenges, from getting customers to leave reviews to creating a referral program in which people wanted to participate. It was a learning curve, figuring out how to effectively implement these strategies and truly engage our customers.

One of the biggest hurdles was simply getting customers to share their experiences. People are busy, and even when they're happy with a service, they might not think to write a review or recommend us to others. We realized we needed to make this process as easy and appealing as possible. We started by sending follow-up emails after a purchase, thanking customers for their business and gently encouraging them to leave feedback. We included direct links to review sites to make it as straightforward as possible. For our referral program, we made sure the incentives were enticing enough to motivate customers to want to share their referral codes.

Another challenge was dealing with negative feedback. It's an inevitable part of doing business, but it was tough not to take it personally at first. We learned to view negative feedback as an opportunity to improve and show our commitment to customer satisfaction. We made it a point to respond to every piece of feedback, positive or negative, and take actionable steps to address any customer-issued issues. This helped us improve our products and services and showed other customers that we were listening and cared about their experiences.

Engaging satisfied customers and turning them into advocates for our brand took time and effort. We found that personal touches made a big difference. For example, sending personalized thank you notes or small gifts to our most loyal customers helped strengthen those relationships. We also created a community around our brand by hosting events and creating spaces online where our customers could connect with each other. This sense of community encouraged more social proof and referrals and made our customers feel valued and appreciated.

Overcoming these challenges wasn't easy, but it was worth it. By addressing these obstacles head-on and finding creative solutions, we built a strong foundation of social proof and a successful referral program. These efforts have paid off in spades, helping us grow our customer base and strengthen our brand through the powerful voices of our satisfied customers.

Wrapping up our journey through the world of social proof and referrals, it's clear these strategies are not just trends but essential elements for success in today's market. From my experience, I've seen firsthand how powerful a well-placed testimonial can be or how a single referral can open doors to a whole new set of customers. It's about trust, credibility, and human connection—elements that remain at the heart of every business transaction.

Starting small was our mantra when we first dipped our toes into leveraging social proof and building our referral program. We didn't have a massive budget or a big team, but we were committed to genuinely connecting with our customers and encouraging them to share their experiences. This approach allowed us to gradually build a robust system of social proof and a referral program that genuinely worked for our business model.

The beauty of starting small is that it gives you room to experiment and refine your strategies. You learn what resonates with your customers and what doesn't, which platforms they prefer, and how they like to be rewarded for their loyalty. This iterative process is invaluable because it ensures that your efforts are always aligned with your customer's evolving needs and preferences.

Investing in social proof and referral strategies has long-term benefits that far outweigh the initial effort and resources required. Not only do they help in acquiring new customers, but they also play a crucial role in building and maintaining a loyal customer base. These strategies contribute to a positive brand image, foster a sense of community among your customers, and drive sustainable business growth.

As we close this chapter, my final thoughts are of optimism and encouragement for other business owners. Embrace the power of social proof and the impact of a well-crafted referral program. Let your satisfied customers be your most vocal advocates, and remember, the journey to building a successful business is a marathon, not a sprint. With patience, persistence, and a willingness to continuously adapt and refine your strategies, the rewards will be well worth the effort.

8

EXECUTION AND SCALING

When it comes to running a business, moving from the drawing board to real-world action is a game-changer. It's one thing to have a plan, but it's entirely another to execute it effectively. This phase, the leap from planning to doing, is where many businesses find their true test. It's not just about having a strategy; it's about bringing that strategy to life to propel your business forward.

Execution is the heartbeat of any business's lifecycle. Without it, the most brilliant plans remain just that—plans. It's the engine that drives growth, transforms ideas into revenue, and dreams into realities. But here's the thing: execution is hard. It demands discipline, flexibility, and an unwavering focus on the end goal. And when it comes to scaling, those challenges multiply.

I've faced my share of hurdles when trying to scale my business. There were moments when it felt like every step forward was met with two steps back. From managing cash flow to keeping the team aligned with the business's evolving needs, each growth phase brought its own set of challenges. Yet, with each obstacle, we learned valuable lessons that helped us overcome immediate issues and strengthened our approach to scaling.

In sharing my journey, I hope to shed light on the realities of scaling a business. It's not always a smooth ride, but with persistence and a solid strategy in place, it's possible to navigate the complexities of growth and achieve long-term success.

SETTING THE STAGE FOR EXECUTION

Getting a plan off the ground and into action starts with making sure your strategy isn't just a list of lofty ideas but a roadmap of achievable goals. It's about breaking down that big vision into clear, manageable, and, most importantly, actionable steps. This process has always been a cornerstone of how I approach business. It's one thing to say we're going to increase sales or improve customer service; it's another to outline exactly how we will do it, step by step.

But having a plan is only half the battle. The real challenge lies in embedding a culture of execution within the team. It's about fostering an environment where everyone understands their role in the bigger picture and is committed to doing their part. In my experience, this involves a lot of communication, setting clear expectations, and providing the support and resources the team needs to succeed. It's about creating a sense of ownership and accountability, where each team member feels responsible for the outcome.

Leadership plays a crucial role in this. As a leader, it's my job to set the direction and inspire and motivate my team to follow. It means being in the trenches with them, celebrating the wins, and learning from the losses. It's about showing resilience in the face of challenges and staying focused on the end goal. Leading by example has always been my mantra. If I expect my team to commit to our goals and work hard to achieve them, I need to show them that I'm just as committed and working as hard, if not harder.

In essence, setting the stage for execution is about aligning our goals, building a culture that values action, and leading in a way that drives us forward. It's these elements that transform plans into results.

BUILDING A COMPETENT TEAM

Building a team that can take your business to the next level is about more than just filling seats. It's about understanding the key roles and skills essential for growth and finding the right people to fill those roles. For me, this meant looking hard at where we were as a company and where we wanted to go. It was clear that to get there, we needed people who were not just skilled but also aligned with our vision and values.

Recruiting the right talent is only part of the equation. Retaining that talent is where the real challenge lies. In my experience, people stay where they feel valued and heard and where they see opportunities for growth. This means creating an environment that encourages feedback, recognizes achievements, and invests in professional development. It's about showing your team that you're not just invested in the business's success but in their success as well.

Creating a team environment that's conducive to innovation and efficiency has been a key focus for us. It's about fostering a culture where new ideas are welcomed and where there's a constant drive to improve. This doesn't happen overnight. It requires consistent effort to build trust, encourage collaboration, and empower your team to take initiative. It's been about leading by example—being open to new ideas, willing to take calculated risks, and always looking for ways to improve things.

In building our team, I've learned that it's not just about the skills and experience people bring to the table. It's about their ability to work together toward a common goal, their willingness to push boundaries, and their commitment to the vision we're all working toward. This combination of talent, teamwork, and shared vision sets the foundation for growth and success.

STREAMLINING OPERATIONS

Streamlining operations has been a game-changer for my business. It all started with a thorough assessment of our processes. I took a step back to look at how we were doing things, questioning every step and looking for ways to do it better. This wasn't about cutting corners but finding smarter, more efficient ways to operate.

Implementing new systems and technologies played a big part in this transformation. For instance, adopting project management software helped us track progress in real time, identify bottlenecks early, and improve team collaboration. It was about leveraging technology to enhance our capabilities, not replace the human element.

Flexibility in operations has been crucial, especially as we began to scale. The strategies and processes that worked when we were smaller didn't necessarily fit as we grew. Being open to change and willing to adapt our operations has allowed us to respond more effectively to new challenges and opportunities. It meant not being too attached to "the way we've always done things" and being willing to evolve.

This approach to streamlining operations has not only made us more efficient but also more resilient. It's allowed us to maintain a high level of service as we grow without compromising on quality or our values. For any business owner looking to scale, I advise starting with your operations. Look for ways to improve, embrace technology, and stay flexible. It's a continuous process that can significantly impact your business's success.

FINANCIAL MANAGEMENT FOR SCALING

Managing cash flow during expansion has been one of the most critical aspects of scaling my business. It's like navigating a rapid river; you must keep moving forward without capsizing. I learned early on that even if sales are booming, you can run into trouble if your cash isn't managed properly. It's not just about having money in the bank; it's about timing, knowing when money will come in and when it needs to go out.

Financing growth was another big lesson for me. So many options exist, from loans to investors to crowdfunding. Each comes with its own set of considerations. I had to weigh the benefits of each against what I was willing to give up, whether it was equity, control, or being in debt. It was about finding the right fit for my business, not just the easiest or quickest source of cash.

Budgeting and financial forecasting for scale have been indispensable tools. I used to think of budgeting as just tracking expenses, but it's so much more. It's about setting a roadmap for where you want your business to go and then making sure you're on track to get there. On the other hand, financial forecasting has allowed me to anticipate future financial needs and challenges, helping me make informed decisions about where to allocate resources.

In all of this, the key has been to stay informed and adaptable. Financial management isn't a set-it-and-forget-it part of the business. It requires constant attention and adjustment, especially during periods of growth. It's a complex dance of managing the money you have, understanding the money you'll need, and making sure you don't stretch yourself too thin. For anyone looking to scale their business, getting a solid handle on financial management is not just helpful; it's essential.

MARKETING AND SALES STRATEGIES FOR GROWTH

When it came to growing my business, I quickly realized that my marketing strategies needed to evolve. Initially, my focus was local, but as we started to scale, I saw the potential for a much broader reach. This meant rethinking not just the platforms we used but also the messaging. We started targeting our ads more strategically, using data to understand where our potential customers were and what they wanted to hear from us. It was a game-changer. Suddenly, we weren't just a local business; we were attracting customers from all over.

Scaling our sales operations was another critical step. Initially, it was just me and a couple of team members handling sales. But as demand grew, we needed a bigger team and a more structured approach. We invested in sales training and built a sales process that could be replicated and scaled. This wasn't just about hiring more people; it was about making sure each new team member could be as effective as possible, as quickly as possible.

Customer retention became even more important as we grew. Getting caught up in the chase for new customers is easy, but I learned that keeping our existing customers happy was just as crucial. We implemented loyalty programs and made customer service a top priority. We also started using customer feedback to guide our product development, ensuring we always met their needs. This focus on retention didn't just keep our existing customers coming back; it also turned them into advocates for our brand, driving even more growth.

In all of this, the key was flexibility. What worked for us at one growth stage wasn't necessarily going to work at the next. We had to be willing to adapt our strategies, learn from our successes and failures, and always keep our eyes on the long-term goal. Growing a business isn't just about increasing sales; it's about building a sustainable operation that can thrive in the long run.

PRODUCT DEVELOPMENT AND INNOVATION

When it comes to growing a business, one of the most exciting parts is developing new products. But it's not just about coming up with ideas that we think are cool; it's about creating products that meet the evolving needs of our market. We spend a lot of time listening to our customers, understanding their challenges, and brainstorming solutions to make their lives easier. This approach has helped us stay relevant and competitive, even as market trends shift.

Encouraging innovation within our team has been key to our product development success. I've always believed that great ideas can come from anywhere, so we've created an environment where everyone feels comfortable sharing their thoughts and suggestions. We hold regular brainstorming sessions and have an open-door policy for new ideas. Seeing the creativity and passion our team brings to these discussions is amazing. This culture of innovation has led to some of our most successful products.

Managing the product lifecycle is also crucial. It's not enough to launch a product and then forget about it. We monitor our products' performance closely, gathering customer feedback to make improvements. We also keep an eye on sales data to understand when a product might be reaching the end of its lifecycle. This allows us to strategically decide when to update, revamp, or retire products. By managing our product lifecycle effectively, we ensure that our portfolio always meets our customers' needs and supports our company's growth.

In all of this, the goal is sustained growth. By aligning our product development with market needs, fostering a culture of innovation, and managing our product lifecycle wisely, we've introduced new products that keep our customers coming back. It's a dynamic process, but it's one that has allowed us to grow and thrive in a competitive landscape.

EXPANDING MARKET REACH

Expanding into new markets has been a game-changer for us. It's not just about selling more products; it's about connecting with new customers and understanding their unique needs. When we first looked beyond our initial customer base, we realized a whole world of opportunity awaited us. But tapping into these new markets required a thoughtful approach.

We started by doing our homework and researching potential markets to understand their demographics, culture, and consumer behavior. This research helped us identify which markets fit our products well and how we could adapt our offerings to meet local needs. It was fascinating to see how different customer segments had different priorities and how we could solve problems we hadn't considered before.

Geographic expansion was another big step. We looked at regions where our products could fill a gap in the market. This wasn't just about shipping products to new locations; it involved understanding local regulations, logistics, and marketing strategies that resonated with local audiences. We learned a lot through trial and error, adjusting our strategies as we gained more insights.

Partnerships and collaborations have also been crucial in our market expansion efforts. We've teamed up with local businesses that share our values and have a strong understanding of the market. These partnerships have been invaluable, providing us with local insights and helping us navigate new territories more effectively. Together, we've made a bigger impact than we could have on our own.

Expanding our market reach has been an exciting journey. It's pushed us to think creatively, adapt our strategies, and learn from each new challenge. By exploring new markets, focusing on strategic geographic and demographic expansion, and building strong partnerships, we've grown our business and reached more customers than ever before.

OVERCOMING SCALING CHALLENGES

Scaling a business is like navigating uncharted waters. You're excited about the journey ahead but aware of the potential storms. Through my experience, I've learned that scaling comes with its unique set of challenges, and overcoming them requires a mix of foresight, flexibility, and a commitment to maintaining the core values of your business.

One of the first hurdles we encountered was the temptation to grow too quickly. It's easy to get caught up in the excitement of expansion, but rapid growth can strain your resources, dilute your brand, and compromise the quality of your product or service. We had to learn to pace ourselves, ensuring our growth was sustainable and aligned with our long-term vision.

We focused on strategic planning and setting realistic goals to manage our growth effectively. This involved detailed market research, financial forecasting, and securing the necessary funding to support our expansion without overextending ourselves. We also invested in technology and systems that could scale with us, ensuring that our infrastructure could handle increased demand.

Maintaining quality and customer satisfaction as we grew was another major concern. It's crucial to remember that your reputation is built on every interaction a customer has with your business. As we expanded, ensuring that our products and services remained consistent and high-quality became a top priority. We implemented rigorous quality control processes and stayed close to our customers, soliciting their feedback and making adjustments based on their insights.

We also recognized the importance of maintaining a strong company culture during periods of rapid growth. It's easy for the essence of what made your business successful in the first place to get diluted as you add new team members and enter new markets. We made a concerted effort to keep our core values at the forefront of everything we do, from hiring practices to daily operations, ensuring that every team member understands and embodies these values.

Overcoming the scaling challenges has been a learning process that has required us to be proactive, resourceful, and patient. By identifying potential pitfalls, strategically managing our growth, and staying true to our commitment to quality and customer satisfaction, we've navigated the complexities of expansion and built a stronger, more resilient business.

MEASURING SUCCESS AND ADJUSTING COURSE

Scaling a business isn't just about growing bigger; it's about growing smarter. That's why measuring success and being willing to adjust our course has been crucial for us. We've leaned heavily on key performance indicators (KPIs) to gauge our progress in this journey. These metrics aren't just numbers on a page; they're the pulse of our business, telling us where we're thriving and where we need to pivot.

For us, some of the most telling KPIs have included customer acquisition cost, customer lifetime value, and employee satisfaction, among others. These indicators help us understand our financial health and how well we're serving our customers and team members. It's a holistic approach to growth that keeps the well-being of our community at the forefront.

But having the data is only part of the equation. The real magic happens in our regular strategy reviews. These aren't just check-ins; they're opportunities to question our assumptions, celebrate our wins, and, most importantly, correct our course when necessary. Here, we've made some of our most impactful decisions, like expanding into new markets or adjusting our product offerings based on customer feedback.

Staying agile has been our mantra, especially in a market that never stands still. We've learned to embrace change not as a threat but as an opportunity. When a new competitor emerges or industry trends shift, we see it as a chance to innovate and improve. This mindset has been key to our ability to scale successfully. It's not just about growing for the sake of growth; it's about evolving to meet the needs of our customers and our team.

In the end, scaling is a continuous journey that requires vigilance, flexibility, and a commitment to constant improvement. By focusing on the right KPIs, regularly reassessing our strategies, and staying adaptable, we've navigated growth challenges and emerged stronger.

The path to growth is both challenging and rewarding. From the outset, we've explored a variety of strategies that are essential for taking a business from its early stages to a larger, more sustainable operation. These strategies, from building a solid team to leveraging technology and managing finances, are the backbone of successful scaling.

But beyond the strategies and tactics, there's a mindset that's crucial for navigating the scaling journey. It's about seeing challenges not as roadblocks but as stepping stones to greater achievements. Every obstacle encountered is an opportunity to learn, adapt, and become stronger. This perspective has guided me, turning potential setbacks into moments of insight and innovation.

Scaling a business is more than just increasing numbers; it's about expanding your vision and impact. It requires a commitment to continuous improvement and a willingness to evolve. The scaling journey is unique for every business owner and is filled with its own highs and lows. Yet, this very journey shapes us, driving us toward building not just a bigger business but a better one.

As we close this chapter, I hope you feel inspired to tackle the challenges of scaling head-on. Remember, the path may not always be smooth, but the lessons learned and the growth achieved along the way are invaluable. Here's to embracing the journey of scaling, with all its complexities and rewards, and moving forward with resilience, creativity, and an unwavering focus on your vision.

CONCLUSION

REFLECTING ON THE JOURNEY

Looking back on the path of growing a business, it's like navigating through a dense forest. There are moments when the trees seem too thick, the path too winding, and the destination too far. I've faced challenges that tested every ounce of my resolve, from financial hurdles to market shifts that demanded quick adaptation. It wasn't just about having a good idea; it was about nurturing that idea, fighting to keep it alive through storms and droughts, and pushing forward even when the end seemed nowhere in sight.

However, this journey isn't just about the obstacles. It's also about the incredible resilience and adaptability that entrepreneurs show. I've seen it in myself and in countless others who've shared this path. A certain kind of strength comes from facing down challenges and emerging on the other side, not just intact but stronger. It's about the late nights, the early mornings, and the unwavering belief that what we're building is worth the effort.

Celebrating this resilience is crucial. Every entrepreneur's journey is a testament to human creativity and determination. We adapt, we learn, and we grow. This adaptability isn't just a skill; it's a testament to our spirit. It makes the entrepreneurial journey not just possible but deeply rewarding.

KEY TAKEAWAYS

Success doesn't hinge on a single factor. It's a mosaic of strategies, each vital in its own right yet powerful only when woven together. Here's a recap of the essential strategies that form the backbone of business success:

1. **Importance of a Clear Business Strategy**: It all starts with a roadmap. A clear business strategy acts as a compass, guiding every decision and action. It's about knowing where you want to go and plotting a course to get there.

2. **Mastery of Financial Fundamentals**: Understanding the numbers is non-negotiable. Mastery of financial fundamentals ensures you can make informed decisions, manage resources wisely, and keep the business financially healthy.

3. **Deep Understanding of the Market**: Knowing your market inside and out enables you to meet your customers where they are. It's about understanding their needs, preferences, and pain points and tailoring your offerings accordingly.

4. **Effective Use of Acquisition Channels and Sales Tactics**: Finding and converting prospects into customers is an art and a science. It requires a mix of the right channels and tactics to reach your audience and compel them to act.

5. **Leveraging Technology and Content for Growth**: In today's digital age, technology and content are indispensable tools for reaching and engaging customers. They're the engines that drive visibility, engagement, and, ultimately, growth.

6. **Prioritizing Customer Retention and Relationship Building**: Acquiring a new customer is just the beginning. The real value lies in keeping them. Prioritizing customer retention and nurturing relationships lead to loyalty, repeat business, and referrals.

7. **The Power of Social Proof and Referrals**: Trust is currency. Social proof and referrals tap into the trust factor, leveraging the voices of satisfied customers to attract new ones.

8. **Execution and Scaling with Precision**: Growth is a deliberate process. It requires precise execution and strategic scaling, ensuring that as the business grows, it remains sustainable and true to its core values.

The interconnectedness of these areas cannot be overstated. Each element feeds into and amplifies the others, creating a synergistic effect that propels the business forward. It's this holistic approach that underpins sustained growth and success.

THE ROLE OF CONTINUOUS LEARNING

In the world of business, standing still is the same as falling behind. That's why I always say that learning never stops. It's not just about getting ahead; it's about staying relevant. As a business owner, I've learned that the landscape around us is always shifting. New technologies emerge, market trends evolve, and customer preferences change. To keep up, we need to stay on our toes, always ready to learn something new.

I encourage every entrepreneur to embrace continuous learning. It's not just about formal education or qualifications. It's about being curious, seeking out new knowledge, and being open to change. This could mean attending workshops, reading industry news, or even listening to feedback from customers and employees. Every piece of information is a chance to learn and improve.

Staying curious and open to change has been a cornerstone of my approach to business. It's easy to get comfortable, especially when things are going well. However, comfort can lead to complacency, and in a fast-paced world, complacency can lead to obsolescence. By fostering a culture of continuous learning within my team, we've been able to adapt quickly, adopting new technologies and strategies that have kept us ahead of the curve.

The role of continuous learning in business cannot be overstated. It's what keeps us agile, innovative, and competitive. I urge my fellow entrepreneurs to stay curious, embrace change, and never stop learning. It's not just about building a successful business; it's about building a resilient one that can withstand the test of time and change.

Looking Ahead

As I look to the future, I see a horizon filled with both challenges and opportunities. The business landscape is like a fast-moving river, always changing, always flowing toward new possibilities. It's exciting, but also means we must be ready for anything. Innovation isn't just a buzzword in my book; it's a survival strategy. Staying ahead of market trends is how we ensure our place in the future of business.

I remember when I first grasped the importance of looking forward, not just to the next quarter, but years later. It was a turning point. I realized that to build something lasting, I had to anticipate changes before they happened. This meant investing in new technologies, even when they seemed like a gamble, and adapting our business model to meet future customer needs, even before they knew what those needs were.

The importance of innovation can't be overstated. It's not about being trendy; it's about being relevant. As the market evolves, so must we. This means constantly questioning the status quo, experimenting with new approaches, and being willing to take calculated risks. It's about creating a culture where new ideas are welcomed, and failure is seen not as a setback but as a step toward success.

Looking ahead, I'm excited about the opportunities that lie before us. Yes, there will be challenges, but with a mindset geared toward innovation and a willingness to adapt, I believe we can not only meet these challenges but turn them into our greatest victories. The future is bright for those willing to lead the charge toward innovation and stay ahead of the curve.

BUILDING A SUPPORTIVE COMMUNITY

Building a supportive community has been a cornerstone of my business-owner journey. It's about more than just networking; it's about creating meaningful relationships with other entrepreneurs who understand the highs and lows of running a business. These connections have been invaluable, offering both support and insight when I've needed it most.

I've learned that we're stronger together. By sharing our experiences, challenges, and successes, we can help each other grow. Early on, I realized the importance of seeking mentors who could guide me through unfamiliar territory. Their wisdom and advice have been instrumental in navigating the complexities of business ownership. But mentorship is a two-way street. As I've gained experience, I've made it a point to give back, sharing my insights with those who are just starting.

This sense of community and mutual support is what keeps us resilient. It's easy to feel isolated in the world of entrepreneurship, but knowing there's a network of peers who are just a phone call or a coffee meet-up away makes all the difference. It's about more than just business; it's about building a community of like-minded individuals committed to lifting each other up.

Invest time in building your community. Seek out mentors, join local business groups, and don't be afraid to share your knowledge. The relationships you build will become one of your most valuable assets, providing business opportunities, friendship, advice, and support as you navigate the path of entrepreneurship.

FINAL WORDS OF ENCOURAGEMENT

As we close this journey together, I want to leave you with a few words of encouragement. Pursuing your business goals is a path filled with both challenges and triumphs. It requires passion, perseverance, and a steadfast belief in your vision. Remember, every setback you encounter is not a sign of failure but a stepping stone toward greater insights and success. The lessons learned from these experiences are invaluable, shaping you into a more resilient and savvy entrepreneur.

Building and growing a business is one of the most rewarding endeavors you can undertake. It's a testament to your courage, creativity, and determination. Yes, there will be days filled with doubt and frustration, but the satisfaction of overcoming obstacles and seeing your vision come to life is unparalleled. The impact you can make on your community, employees, and life is profound.

I urge you to apply the insights and strategies in this book to your business journey. Remember, you're not alone in this. There's a whole community of entrepreneurs, each with unique experiences and wisdom to share. Reach out, engage, and become an active participant in this community. Share your story, listen to others, and find solace that we're all navigating this path together.

As you turn the page on this chapter and look toward the future, do so with an open heart and an eager mind. The world of entrepreneurship is dynamic and ever-changing, offering endless opportunities for growth and innovation. Embrace it with both hands, and never lose sight of why you started this journey in the first place.

Let's continue to support each other, share our successes, and learn from our setbacks. Together, we can achieve remarkable things. Here's to your success, and may your business journey be as fulfilling as it is prosperous.

Work Less and Make More Money Than Ever Before

Take your business to the next level
with a fresh perspective.

These insights show you exactly how to break
through plateaus and achieve big profits.

Go beyond your expectations and
see what's possible for your business.

jetlaunch.link/sab2

www.ingramcontent.com/pod-product-compliance
Lightning Source LLC
Chambersburg PA
CBHW031401180326
41458CB00043B/6554/J